Those Amazing Electronic Thinking Machines!

THOSE AMAZING ELECTRONIC THINKING MACHINES!

An Anthology of Robot and Computer Stories

Edited by
Isaac Asimov
Martin S. Greenberg
Charles H. Waugh

A GROLIER COMPANY

FRANKLIN WATTS / 1983
NEW YORK / LONDON / TORONTO / SYDNEY

Library of Congress Cataloging in Publication Data
Main entry under title:

Those amazing electronic thinking machines!

Summary: Nine science fiction stories by the
likes of Isaac Asimov and Arthur C. Clarke,
featuring robots and computers.
1. Computers—Juvenile fiction.
2. Science fiction. 3. Short stories.
[1. Computers—Fiction.
2. Science fiction. 3. Short stories]
I. Asimov, Isaac, 1920–
II. Greenberg, Martin, 1918–
III. Waugh, Charles.
PZ5.T37 1983   [Fic]   83-5956
ISBN   0-531-04667-2

Asimov—Copyright © 1953 by Ziff-Davis Publishing Co.; copyright renewed © 1980 by Isaac Asimov. Reprinted by permission of the author.

Hickey—Copyright © 1952 by Ziff-Davis Publishing Co. Reprinted by arrangement with Holding Agent Forrest J. Ackerman, 2495 Glendower Ave., Hollywood, CA 90027. Author's estate please contact.

Del Rey—Copyright © 1964 by Galaxy Publishing Corporation. Reprinted by permission of the author and his agents, the Scott Meredith Literary Agency, Inc., 845 Third Ave., New York, NY 10022.

Laumer ("Prototaph")—Copyright © 1966 by Condé Nast Publications, Inc. Reprinted by permission of Robert P. Mills, Ltd.

Clarke—Copyright © 1965 by HMH Publishing Corporation. Reprinted by permission of the author and his agents, the Scott Meredith Literary Agency, Inc., 845 Third Ave., New York, NY 10022.

Kubilius—Copyright © 1951 by Fictioneers, Inc. Reprinted by arrangement with Holding Agent Forrest J. Ackerman, 2495 Glendower Ave., Hollywood, CA 90027. Author please contact.

Dickson—Copyright © 1965 by Condé Nast Publications, Inc. Reprinted by permission of the author.

Laumer ("Placement Test")—Copyright © 1964 by Ziff-Davis Publishing Co. Reprinted by permission of Robert P. Mills, Ltd.

Brown—Copyright © 1954 by Fredric Brown. Reprinted by permission of International Creative Management, Inc.

Contents

Those Amazing Electronic Thinking Machines!

INTRODUCTION
Isaac Asimov

Throughout all of history, human beings have been able to exchange ideas by way of the spoken word only with other human beings. Intelligence of the human sort has existed only in ourselves.

This, it seems, has made us feel rather lonely. And so we have created many myths and legends that contain speaking beings who are not human.

In the Bible, for instance, there are two speaking animals. In Chapter 3 of Genesis, there is the serpent who speaks to Eve and persuades her to eat fruit from the tree of knowledge of good and evil. In Chapter 22 of the Book of Numbers, the donkey on which the wizard, Balaam, rides is given the power of speech, in order that it might protest being beaten for trying to avoid an angel that blocked its path, an angel Balaam himself does not see.

In Homer's *Iliad,* which the ancient Greeks revered as many modern Westerners revere the Bible, the Greek warrior, Achilles, had horses that were divine and immortal. As he prepared for the final battle in the epic, one of his horses spoke and warned Achilles that he would survive the battle but die soon after.

Animals that think like human beings and exchange ideas in human fashion are found in all sorts of folktales, from Grimm to *Uncle Remus.* Even modern storytellers think up such tales, as Hugh Lofting did in his *Dr. Dolittle* books and Richard Adams did in *Watership Down.*

In addition, all sorts of fanciful creatures of human or even superhuman intelligence have been invented. Fairies and elves have been thought to inhabit the earth with us at various times, and demons, nymphs, and monsters of many sorts were thought to surround us.

Nowadays, though, we are more skeptical. We are aware that there is no conclusive evidence of any nonhuman intelligence among us. Animals do not truly speak. Even parrots and myna birds, which can mimic human sound, do not understand what they are saying. Chimpanzees and gorillas may be able to communicate simple ideas in sign language, but they can't go very far in this direction. Dolphins may have a language of their own, but as yet we have no way of understanding it. And as for spirits, monsters, demons, and fairies—nonsense!

So human beings—with their large brains, the ideas those brains invent, and the speech that communicates those ideas—remain alone on this planet.

It may be that there are other intelligences equal to (or even superior to) our own on planets orbiting stars other than the sun. (Many astronomers think this must be so.) But we have no evidence for this, either. If extraterrestrial intelligences exist, we have not heard from them or detected them.

Well, then, are we condemned to intellectual loneliness forever?

Not at all, for human beings have set about creating thinking machines. Scientists and engineers are designing nonhuman brains and building devices that have "artificial intelligence."

The notion of human beings actually constructing something that can think is an old one. There is the medieval legend of the Golem, for example, and the modern tale of the Monster built by Dr. Frankenstein. These, however, were just exercises of the imagination.

The first person to think of a legitimate way to construct a machine that could do some of the things that until then only thinking human beings could do was an English mathematician named Charles Babbage. About a century and a half ago, Babbage tried to build a machine that would be capable of solving mathematical problems. Unfortunately, all he had to work with were mechanical devices—wheels, gears, levers, and so on. He tried for many years, but he could never get his machine to work as he wished. Eventually, he ran out of money and had to abandon the project.

By World War II, however, scientists had electronic devices to play with, and these could do the job much more quickly and elegantly than mechanical devices could. In 1946, the first electronic computer, ENIAC, was built, and in the forty years since, rapid advances have made computers capable of conducting ever more complicated operations while growing smaller and smaller.

In the middle 1970s, switching devices were down to microscopic size (the "computer-on-a-chip"), and it was possible to have very complex computers so small that you could slip one into your pocket, and so cheap that almost everyone could have one.

Today, everything is becoming computerized. Authors are writing on computerized word-processors. Computerized automobiles are being built by computerized industrial robots. Children are playing with video games that have computers for brains. In fact, video games have become a multibillion-dollar industry.

What if computers grow to be as intelligent, in their own way, as human beings are? Or even more intelligent? Maybe they will be like some of the nonhuman intelligences we imagined in our legends. In that case, will they work for us or against us?

Will advanced computers try to save us, as the donkey tried to save Balaam? Or will they try to harm us, as the serpent tried to harm Eve? Will computers be helpful elves or spiteful goblins?

We don't know, really, but we can imagine. In this anthology are science fiction stories that deal with what might happen if computers grow much more capable than they already are.

One widespread fear seems to be that computers might get out of human control. Well, might they? And if they do, how will we stop them? Think about it, then read the stories contained here to see what some others have thought about those amazing electronic thinking machines.

SALLY
Isaac Asimov

No one loves cars more than Americans. Most of us can hardly wait until we are old enough to drive, even though the costs of owning and operating an automobile are great. In "Sally," Isaac Asimov poses two interesting questions. What would happen if a car could think? And what would happen if it could *feel?*

Sally was coming down the lake road, so I waved to her and called her by name. I always liked to see Sally. I liked all of them, you understand, but Sally's the prettiest one of the lot. There just isn't any question about it.

She moved a little faster when I waved to her. Nothing undignified. She was never that. She moved just enough faster to show that she was glad to see me, too.

I turned to the man standing beside me. "That's Sally," I said.

He smiled at me and nodded.

Mrs. Hester had brought him in. She said, "This is Mr. Gellhorn, Jake. You remember he sent you the letter asking for an appointment."

That was just talk, really. I have a million things to do around the Farm, and one thing I just can't waste my time on is mail. That's why I have Mrs. Hester around. She lives pretty close by, she's good at attending to foolishness without running to me about it, and most of all, she likes Sally and the rest. Some people don't.

"Glad to see you, Mr. Gellhorn," I said.

"Raymond J. Gellhorn," he said, and gave me his hand, which I shook and gave back.

He was a largish fellow, half a head taller than I and wider, too. He was about half my age, thirtyish. He had black hair, plastered down slick, with a part in the middle, and a thin mustache, very neatly trimmed. His jawbones got big under his ears and made him look as if he had a slight case of mumps. On video he'd be a natural to play the villain, so I assumed he was a nice fellow. It goes to show that video can't be wrong all the time.

"I'm Jacob Folkers," I said. "What can I do for you?"

He grinned. It was a big, wide, white-toothed grin. "You can tell me a little about your Farm here, if you don't mind."

I heard Sally coming up behind me and I put out my hand. She slid right into it and the feel of the hard, glossy enamel of her fender was warm in my palm.

"A nice automatobile," said Gellhorn.

That's one way of putting it. Sally was a 2045 convertible with a Hennis-Carleton positronic motor and an Armat chassis. She had the cleanest, finest lines I've ever seen on any model, bar none. For five years, she'd been my favorite, and I'd put everything into her I could dream up. In all that time, there'd never been a human being behind her wheel.

Not once.

"Sally," I said, patting her gently, "meet Mr. Gellhorn."

Sally's cylinder-purr keyed up a little. I listened carefully for any knocking. Lately, I'd been hearing motor-knock in almost all the cars and changing the gasoline hadn't done a bit of good. Sally was as smooth as her paint job this time, however.

"Do you have names for all your cars?" asked Gellhorn.

He sounded amused, and Mrs. Hester doesn't like people to sound as though they are making fun of the Farm. She said, sharply, "Certainly. The cars have real personalities, don't they, Jake? The sedans are all males and the convertibles are females."

Gellhorn was smiling again. "And do you keep them in separate garages, ma'am?"

Mrs. Hester glared at him.

Gellhorn said to me, "And now I wonder if I can talk to you alone, Mr. Folkers?"

"That depends," I said. "Are you a reporter?"

"No, sir. I'm a sales agent. Any talk we have is not for publication. I assure you I am interested in strict privacy."

"Let's walk down the road a bit. There's a bench we can use."

We started down. Mrs. Hester walked away. Sally nudged along after us.

I said, "You don't mind if Sally comes along, do you?"

"Not at all. She can't repeat what we say, can she?" He laughed at his own joke, reached over and rubbed Sally's grille.

Sally raced her motor and Gellhorn's hand drew away quickly.

"She's not used to strangers," I explained.

We sat down on the bench under the big oak tree where we could look across the small lake to the private speedway. It was the warm part of the day and the cars were out in force, at least thirty of them. Even at this distance I could see that Jeremiah was pulling his usual stunt of sneaking up behind some staid older model, then putting on a jerk of speed and yowling past with deliberately squealing brakes. Two weeks before he had crowded old Angus off the asphalt altogether, and I had turned off his motor for two days.

It didn't help, though, I'm afraid, and it looks as though there's nothing to be done about it. Jeremiah is a sports model to begin with and that kind is awfully hot-headed.

"Well, Mr. Gellhorn," I said. "Could you tell me why you want the information?"

But he was just looking around. He said, "This *is* an amazing place, Mr. Folkers."

"I wish you'd call me Jake. Everyone does."

"All right, Jake. How many cars do you have here?"

"Fifty-one. We get one or two new ones every year. One year we got five. We haven't lost one yet. They're all in perfect running order. We even have a '15 model Mat-O-Mot in working order. One of the original automatics. It was the first car here."

Good old Matthew. He stayed in the garage most of the day now, but then he was the grandaddy of all positronic-motored cars. Those were the days when blind war veterans, paraplegics and heads of state were the only ones who drove automatics. But Samson Harridge was my boss, and he was rich enough to be able to get one. I was his chauffeur at the time.

The thought makes me feel old. I can remember when there wasn't an automobile in the world with brains enough to find its own way home. I chauffeured dead lumps of machines that needed a man's hand at their controls every minute. Every year machines like that used to kill tens of thousands of people.

The automatics fixed that. A positronic brain can react much faster than a human one, of course, and it paid people to keep hands off the controls. You got in, punched your destination and let it go its own way.

We take it for granted now, but I remember when the first laws came out forcing the old machines off the highways and limiting travel to automatics. Lord, what a fuss. They called it everything from communism to fascism, but it emptied the highways and stopped the killing, and still more people get around more easily the new way.

Of course, the automatics were ten to a hundred times as expensive as the hand-driven ones, and there weren't many that could afford a private vehicle. The industry specialized in turning out omnibus-automatics. You could always call a company and have one stop at your door in a matter of minutes and take you where you wanted to go. Usually, you had to drive with others who were going your way, but what's wrong with that?

Samson Harridge had a private car though, and I went to him the minute it arrived. The car wasn't Matthew to me then. I didn't know it was going to be the dean of the Farm some day. I only knew it was taking my job away and I hated it.

I said, "You won't be needing me any more, Mr. Harridge?"

He said, "What are you dithering about, Jake? You don't think I'll trust myself to a contraption like that, do you? You stay right at the controls."

I said, "But it works by itself, Mr. Harridge. It scans the road, reacts properly to obstacles, humans, and other cars, and remembers routes to travel."

"So they say. So they say. Just the same, you're sitting right behind the wheel in case anything goes wrong."

Funny how you can get to like a car. In no time I was calling it Matthew and was spending all my time keeping it polished and humming. A positronic brain stays in condition best when it's got control of its chassis at all times, which means it's worth keeping the gas tank filled so that the motor can turn over slowly day and night. After a while, it got so I could tell by the sound of the motor how Matthew felt.

In his own way, Harridge grew fond of Matthew, too. He had no one else to like. He'd divorced or outlived three wives and outlived five children and three grandchildren. So when he died, maybe it wasn't surprising that he had his estate converted into a Farm for Retired Automobiles, with me in charge and Matthew the first member of a distinguished line.

It's turned out to be my life. I never got married. You can't get married and still tend to automatics the way you should.

The newspapers thought it was funny, but after a while they

stopped joking about it. Some things you can't joke about. Maybe you've never been able to afford an automatic and maybe you never will, either, but take it from me, you get to love them. They're hard-working and affectionate. It takes a man with no heart to mistreat one or to see one mistreated.

It got so that after a man had an automatic for a while, he would make provisions for having it left to the Farm, if he didn't have an heir he could rely on to give it good care.

I explained that to Gellhorn.

He said, "Fifty-one cars! That represents a lot of money."

"Fifty thousand minimum per automatic, original investment," I said. "They're worth a lot more now. I've done things for them."

"It must take a lot of money to keep up the Farm."

"You're right there. The Farm's a non-profit organization, which gives us a break on taxes and, of course, new automatics that come in usually have trust funds attached. Still, costs are always going up. I have to keep the place landscaped; I keep laying down new asphalt and keeping the old in repair; there's gasoline, oil, repairs, and new gadgets. It adds up."

"And you've spent a long time at it."

"I sure have, Mr. Gellhorn. Thirty-three years."

"You don't seem to be getting much out of it yourself."

"I don't? You surprise me, Mr. Gellhorn. I've got Sally and fifty others. Look at her."

I was grinning. I couldn't help it. Sally was so clean, it almost hurt. Some insect must have died on her windshield or one speck of dust too many had landed, so she was going to work. A little tube protruded and spurted Tergosol over the glass. It spread quickly over the silicone surface film and squeejees snapped into place instantly, passing over the windshield and forcing the water into the little channel that led it, dripping, down to the ground. Not a speck of water got onto her glistening apple-green hood. Squeejee and detergent tube snapped back into place and disappeared.

Gellhorn said, "I never saw an automatic do that."

"I guess not," I said. "I fixed that up specially on our cars. They're clean. They're always scrubbing their glass. They like it. I've even got Sally fixed up with wax jets. She polishes herself every night till you can see your face in any part of her and shave by it. If I can scrape up the money, I'll be putting it on the rest of the girls. Convertibles are very vain."

"I can tell you how to scrape up the money, if that interests you."

"That always does. How?"

"Isn't it obvious, Jake? Any of your cars is worth fifty thousand minimum, you said. I'll bet most of them top six figures."

"So?"

"Ever think of selling a few?"

I shook my head. "You don't realize it, I guess, Mr. Gellhorn, but I can't sell any of these. They belong to the Farm, not to me."

"The money would go to the Farm."

"The incorporation papers of the Farm provide that the cars receive perpetual care. They can't be sold."

"What about the motors, then?"

"I don't understand you."

Gellhorn shifted position and his voice got confidential. "Look here, Jake, let me explain the situation. There's a big market for private automatics if they could only be made cheaply enough. Right?"

"That's no secret."

"And ninety-five percent of the cost is the motor. Right? Now, I know where we can get a supply of bodies. I also know where we can sell automatics at a good price—twenty or thirty thousand for the cheaper models, maybe fifty or sixty for the better ones. All I need are the motors. You see the solution?"

"I don't, Mr. Gellhorn." I did, but I wanted him to spell it out.

"It's right here. You've got fifty-one of them. You're an expert automatobile mechanic, Jake. You must be. You could unhook a motor and place it in another car so that no one would know the difference."

"It wouldn't be exactly ethical."

"You wouldn't be harming the cars. You'd be doing them a favor. Use your older cars. Use that old Mat-O-Mot."

"Well, now, wait a while, Mr. Gellhorn. The motors and bodies aren't two separate items. They're a single unit. Those motors are used to their own bodies. They just wouldn't be happy in another car."

"All right, that's a point. That's a very good point, Jake. It would be like taking your mind and putting it in someone else's skull, right? You don't think you would like that?"

"I don't think I would. No."

"But what if I took your mind and put it into the body of a young athlete. What about that, Jake? You're not a youngster anymore. If you had the chance, wouldn't you enjoy being twenty again? That's what I'm offering some of your positronic motors. They'll be put into new '57 bodies. The latest construction."

I laughed. "That doesn't make much sense, Mr. Gellhorn. Some of our cars may be old, but they're well-cared for. Nobody drives them. They're allowed their own way. They're *retired,* Mr. Gellhorn. I wouldn't want a twenty-year-old body if it meant I had to dig ditches for the rest of my new life and never have enough to eat.... What do you think, Sally?"

Sally's two doors opened and then shut with a cushioned slam.

"What's that?" said Gellhorn.

"That's the way Sally laughs."

Gellhorn forced a smile. I guess he thought I was making a bad joke. He said, "Talk sense, Jake. Cars are *made* to be driven. They're probably not happy if you don't drive them."

I said, "Sally hasn't been driven in five years. She looks happy to me."

"I wonder."

He got up and walked toward Sally slowly. "Hi, Sally, how'd you like a drive?"

Sally's motor revved up. She backed away.

"Don't push her, Mr. Gellhorn," I said. "She's liable to be a little skittish."

Two sedans were about a hundred yards up the road. They had stopped. Maybe, in their own way, they were watching. I didn't bother about them. I had my eyes on Sally, and I kept them there.

Gellhorn said, "Steady now, Sally." He lunged out and seized the door handle. It didn't budge, of course.

He said, "It opened a minute ago."

I said, "Automatic lock. She's got a sense of privacy, Sally has."

He let go, then said, slowly and deliberately, "A car with a sense of privacy shouldn't go around with its top down."

He stepped back three or four paces, then quickly, so quickly I couldn't take a step to stop him, he ran forward and vaulted into the car. He caught Sally completely by surprise, because as he came down, he shut off the ignition before she could lock it in place.

For the first time in five years, Sally's motor was dead.

I think I yelled, but Gellhorn had the switch on "Manual" and locked that in place, too. He kicked the motor into action. Sally was alive again but she had no freedom of action.

He started up the road. The sedans were still there. They turned and drifted away, not very quickly. I suppose it was all a puzzle to them.

One was Giuseppe, from the Milan factories, and the other was Stephen. They were always together. They were both new at the Farm, but they'd been here long enough to know that our cars just didn't have drivers.

Gellhorn went straight on, and when the sedans finally got it through their heads that Sally wasn't going to slow down, that she *couldn't* slow down, it was too late for anything but desperate measures.

They broke for it, one to each side, and Sally raced between them like a streak. Steve crashed through the lakeside fence and rolled to a halt on the grass and mud not six inches from the water's edge. Giuseppe bumped along the land side of the road to a shaken halt.

I had Steve back on the highway and was trying to find out what harm, if any, the fence had done him, when Gellhorn came back.

Gellhorn opened Sally's door and stepped out. Leaning back, he shut off the ignition a second time.

"There," he said. "I think I did her a lot of good."

I held my temper. "Why did you dash through the sedans? There was no reason for that."

"I kept expecting them to turn out."

"They did. One went through a fence."

"I'm sorry, Jake," he said. "I thought they'd move more quickly. You know how it is. I've been in lots of buses, but I've only been in a private automatic two or three times in my life, and this is the first time I ever drove one. That just shows you, Jake. It got me, driving one, and I'm pretty hard-boiled. I tell you, we don't have to go more than twenty percent below list price to reach a good market, and it would be ninety per cent profit."

"Which we would split?"

"Fifty-fifty. And I take all the risks, remember."

"All right. I listened to you. Now you listen to me." I raised my voice because I was just too mad to be polite anymore. "When you turn off Sally's motor, you hurt her. How would you like to be kicked unconscious? That's what you do to Sally, when you turn her off."

"You're exaggerating, Jake. The automatobuses get turned off every night."

"Sure, that's why I want none of my boys or girls in your fancy '57 bodies, where I won't know what treatment they'll get. Buses need major repairs in their positronic circuits every couple of years. Old Matthew hasn't had his circuits touched in twenty years. What can you offer him compared with that?"

"Well, you're excited now. Suppose you think over my proposition when you've cooled down and get in touch with me."

"I've thought it over all I want to. If I ever see you again, I'll call the police."

His mouth got hard and ugly. "Just a minute, old-timer."

I said, "Just a minute, you. This is private property and I'm ordering you off."

He shrugged. "Well, then, goodbye."

I said, "Mrs. Hester will see you off the property. Make that goodbye permanent."

But it wasn't permanent. I saw him again two days later. Two and a half days, rather, because it was about noon when I saw him first and a little after midnight when I saw him again.

I sat up in bed when he turned the light on, blinking blindly till I made out what was happening. Once I could see, it didn't take much explaining. In fact, it took none at all. He had a gun in his right fist, the nasty little needle barrel just visible between two fingers. I knew that all he had to do was to increase the pressure of his hand and I would be torn apart.

He said, "Put on your clothes, Jake."

I didn't move. I just watched him.

He said, "Look, Jake, I know the situation. I visited you two days ago, remember. You have no guards on this place, no electrified fences, no warning signals. Nothing."

I said, "I don't need any. Meanwhile there's nothing to stop you from leaving, Mr. Gellhorn. I would if I were you. This place can be very dangerous."

He laughed a little. "It is, for anyone on the wrong side of a fist gun."

"I see it," I said. "I know you've got one."

"Then get a move on. My men are waiting."

"No, sir, Mr. Gellhorn. Not unless you tell me what you want, and probably not then."

"I made you a proposition day before yesterday."

"The answer's still no."

"There's more to the proposition now. I've come here with some men and an automatobus. You have your chance to come with me and disconnect twenty-five of the positronic motors. I don't care which twenty-five you choose. We'll load them on the bus and take them away. Once they're disposed of, I'll see to it that you get your fair share of the money."

"I have your word on that, I suppose."

He didn't act as if he thought I was being sarcastic. He said, "You have."

I said, "No."

"If you insist on saying no, we'll go about it in our own way. I'll disconnect the motors myself, only I'll disconnect all fifty-one. Every one of them."

"It isn't easy to disconnect positronic motors, Mr. Gellhorn. Are you a robotics expert? Even if you are, you know, these motors have been modified by me."

"I know that, Jake. And to be truthful, I'm not an expert. I may ruin quite a few motors trying to get them out. That's why I'll have to work over all fifty-one if you don't cooperate. You see, I may only end up with twenty-five when I'm through. The first few I'll tackle will probably suffer the most. Till I get the hang of it, you see. And if I go it myself, I think I'll put Sally first in line."

I said, "I can't believe you're serious, Mr. Gellhorn."

He said, "I'm serious, Jake." He let it all dribble in. "If you want to help, you can keep Sally. Otherwise, she's liable to be hurt very badly. Sorry."

I said, "I'll come with you, but I'll give you one more warning. You'll be in trouble, Mr. Gellhorn."

He thought that was very funny. He was laughing very quietly as we went down the stairs together.

There was an automatobus waiting outside the driveway to the garage apartments. The shadows of three men waited beside it, and their flash beams went on as we approached.

Gellhorn said in a low voice, "I've got the old fellow. Come on. Move the truck up the drive and let's get started."

One of the others leaned in and punched the proper instructions on the control panel. We moved up the driveway with the bus following submissively.

"It won't go inside the garage," I said. "The door won't take it. We don't have buses here. Only private cars."

"All right," said Gellhorn. "Pull it over onto the grass and keep it out of sight."

I could hear the thrumming of the cars when we were still ten yards from the garage.

Usually they quieted down if I entered the garage. This time they didn't. I think they knew that strangers were about, and once the faces of Gellhorn and the others were visible they got noisier. Each motor was a warm rumble, and each motor was knocking irregularly until the place rattled.

The lights went up automatically as we stepped inside. Gellhorn didn't seem bothered by the car noise, but the three men with him looked surprised and uncomfortable. They had the look of the hired thug about them, a look that was not compounded of physical features so much as of a certain wariness of eye and hang-dogness of face. I knew the type and I wasn't worried.

One of them said, "Damn it, they're burning gas."

"My cars always do," I replied stiffly.

"Not tonight," said Gellhorn. "Turn them off."

"It's not that easy, Mr. Gellhorn," I said.

"Get started!" he said.

I stood there. He had his fist gun pointed at me steadily. I said, "I told you, Mr. Gellhorn, that my cars have been well-treated while they've been at the Farm. They're used to being treated that way, and they resent anything else."

"You have one minute. "Lecture me some other time."

"I'm trying to explain something. I'm trying to explain that my cars can understand what I say to them. A positronic motor will learn to do that with time and patience. My cars have learned. Sally understood your proposition two days ago. You'll remember she laughed when I asked her opinion. She also knows what you did to her and so do the two sedans you scattered. And the rest know what to do about trespassers in general."

"Look, you crazy old fool—"

"All I have to say is—" I raised my voice. "Get them!"

One of the men turned pasty and yelled, but his voice was drowned completely in the sound of fifty-one horns turned loose at once. They held their notes, and within the four walls of the garage the echoes rose to a wild, metallic call. Two cars rolled forward, not hurriedly, but with no possible mistake as to their target. Two cars fell in line behind the first two. All the cars were stirring in their separate stalls.

The thugs stared, then backed.

I shouted, "Don't get up against a wall."

Apparently, they had that instinctive thought themselves. They rushed madly for the door of the garage.

At the door, one of Gellhorn's men turned and brought up a fist gun of his own. The needle pellet tore a thin, blue flash toward the first car. The car was Giuseppe.

A thin line of paint peeled up Giuseppe's hood, and the right half of his windshield crazed and splintered but did not break through.

The men were out the door, running, and two by two the cars crunched out after them into the night, their horns calling the charge.

I kept my hand on Gellhorn's elbow, but I don't think he could have moved in any case. His lips were trembling.

I said, "That's why I don't need electrified fences or guards. My property protects itself."

Gellhorn's eyes swiveled back and forth in fascination as, pair by pair, they whizzed by. He said, "They're killers!"

"Don't be silly. They won't kill your men."

"They're killers!"

"They'll just give your men a lesson. My cars have been specially trained for cross-country pursuit for just such an occasion; I think what your men will get will be worse than an outright quick kill. Have you ever been chased by an automatobile?"

Gellhorn didn't answer.

I went on. I didn't want him to miss a thing. "They'll be shadows going no faster than your men, chasing them here, blocking them there, blaring at them, dashing at them, missing with a screech of brake and a thunder of motor. They'll keep it up till your men drop, out of breath and half-dead, waiting for the wheels to crunch over their breaking bones. The cars won't do that. They'll turn away. You can bet, though, that your men will never return here in their lives. Not for all the money you or ten like you could give them. Listen—"

I tightened my hold on his elbow. He strained to hear.

I said, "Don't you hear car doors slamming?"

It was faint and distant, but unmistakable.

I said, "They're laughing. They're enjoying themselves."

His face crumpled with rage. He lifted his hand. He was still holding his fist gun.

I said, "I wouldn't. One automatocar is still with us."

I don't think he had noticed Sally till then. She had moved up so quietly. Though her right front fender nearly touched me, I couldn't hear her motor. She might have been holding her breath.

Gellhorn yelled.

I said, "She won't touch you, as long as I'm with you. But if you kill me.... You know, Sally doesn't like you."

Gellhorn turned the gun in Sally's direction.

"Her motor is shielded," I said, "and before you could ever squeeze the gun a second time she would be on top of you."

"All right, then," he yelled, and suddenly my arm was bent behind my back and twisted so I could hardly stand. He held me between Sally and himself, and his pressure didn't let up. "Back out with me and don't try to break loose, old-timer, or I'll tear your arm out of its socket."

I had to move. Sally nudged along with us, worried, uncertain what to do. I tried to say something to her and couldn't. I could only clench my teeth and moan.

Gellhorn's automatobus was still standing outside the garage. I was forced in. Gellhorn jumped in after me, locking the doors.

He said, "All right, now. We'll talk sense."

I was rubbing my arm, trying to get life back into it, and even as I did I was automatically and without any conscious effort studying the control board of the bus.

I said, "This is a rebuilt job."

"So?" he said caustically. "It's a sample of my work. I picked up a discarded chassis, found a brain I could use and spliced me a private bus. What of it?"

I tore at the repair panel, forcing it aside.

He said, "What the hell. Get away from that." The side of his palm came down numbingly on my left shoulder.

I struggled with him. "I don't want to do this bus any harm. What kind of a person do you think I am? I just want to take a look at some of the motor connections."

It didn't take much of a look. I was boiling when I turned to him. I said, "You're a rotten person. You had no right installing this motor yourself. Why didn't you get a robotics man?"

He said, "Do I look crazy?"

"Even if it was a stolen motor, you had no right to treat it so. I wouldn't treat a man the way you treated that motor. Solder, tape, and pinch clamps! It's brutal!"

"It works, doesn't it?"

"Sure it works, but it must be hell for the bus. You could live with migraine headaches and acute arthritis, but it wouldn't be much of a life. This car is *suffering.*"

"Shut up!" For a moment he glanced out the window at Sally, who had rolled up as close to the bus as she could. He made sure the doors and windows were locked.

He said, "We're getting out of here now, before the other cars come back. We'll stay away."

"How will that help you?"

"Your cars will run out of gas someday, won't they? You haven't got them fixed up so they can tank up on their own, have you? We'll come back and finish the job."

"They'll be looking for me," I said. "Mrs. Hester will call the police."

He was past reasoning with. He just punched the bus in gear. It lurched forward. Sally followed.

He giggled. "What can she do if you're here with me?"

Sally seemed to realize that, too. She picked up speed, passed us and was gone. Gellhorn opened the window next to him and spat through the opening.

The bus lumbered on over the dark road, its motor rattling

unevenly. Gellhorn dimmed the periphery light until the phosphorescent green stripe down the middle of the highway, sparkling in the moonlight, was all that kept us out of the trees. There was virtually no traffic. Two cars passed ours, going the other way, and there was none at all on our side of the highway, either before or behind.

I heard the door-slamming first. Quick and sharp in the silence, first on the right and then on the left. Gellhorn's hands quivered as he punched savagely for increased speed. A beam of light shot out from among a scrub of trees, blinding us. Another beam plunged at us from behind the guard rails on the other side. At a crossover, four hundred yards ahead, there was a sque-e-e-e-e as a car darted across our path.

"Sally went for the rest," I said. "I think you're surrounded."

"So what? What can they do?"

He hunched over the controls, peering through the windshield.

"And don't *you* try anything, old-timer," he muttered.

I couldn't. I was bone-weary; my left arm was on fire. The motor sounds gathered and grew closer. I could hear the motors missing in odd patterns; suddenly it seemed to me that my cars were speaking to one another.

A medley of horns came from behind. I turned and Gellhorn looked quickly into the rear-view mirror. A dozen cars were following in both lanes.

Gellhorn yelled and laughed madly.

I cried, "Stop! Stop the car!"

Because not a quarter of a mile ahead, plainly visible in the light beams of two sedans on the roadside was Sally, her trim body plunked square across the road. Two cars shot into the opposite lane to our left, keeping perfect time with us and preventing Gellhorn from turning out.

But he had no intention of turning out. He put his finger on the full-speed-ahead button and kept it there.

He said, "There'll be no bluffing here. This bus outweighs her five to one, old-timer, and we'll just push her off the road like a dead kitten."

I knew he could. The bus was on manual and his finger was on the button. I knew he would.

I lowered the window, and stuck my head out. "Sally," I screamed. "Get out of the way. *Sally!*"

It was drowned out in the agonized squeal of maltreated brakebands. I felt myself thrown forward and heard Gellhorn's breath puff out of his body.

I said, "What happened?" It was a foolish question. We had stopped. That was what had happened. Sally and the bus were five feet apart. With five times her weight tearing down on her, she had not budged. The guts of her.

Gellhorn yanked at the Manual toggle switch. "It's got to," he kept muttering. "It's got to."

I said, "Not the way you hooked up the motor, expert. Any of the circuits could cross over."

He looked at me with a tearing anger and growled deep in his throat. His hair was matted over his forehead. He lifted his fist.

"That's all the advice out of you there'll ever be, old-timer."

And I knew the needle gun was about to fire.

I pressed back against the bus door, watching the fist come up, and when the door opened I went over backward and out, hitting the ground with a thud. I heard the door slam closed again.

I got to my knees and looked up in time to see Gellhorn struggle uselessly with the closing window, then aim his fist-gun quickly through the glass. He never fired. The bus got under way with a tremendous roar, and Gellhorn lurched backward.

Sally wasn't in the way any longer, and I watched the bus's rear lights flicker away down the highway.

I was exhausted. I sat down right there, right on the highway, and put my head down in my crossed arms, trying to catch my breath.

I heard a car stop gently at my side. When I looked up, it was Sally. Slowly—lovingly, you might say—her front door opened.

No one had driven Sally for five years—except Gellhorn, of course—and I knew how valuable such freedom was to a car. I appreciated the gesture, but I said, "Thanks, Sally, but I'll take one of the newer cars."

I got up and turned away, but skillfully and neatly as a pirouette, she wheeled before me again. I couldn't hurt her feelings. I got in. Her front seat had the fine, fresh scent of an automatobile that kept itself spotlessly clean. I lay down across it, thankfully, and with even, silent, and rapid efficiency, my boys and girls brought me home.

Mrs. Hester brought me the copy of the radio transcript the next evening with great excitement.

"It's Mr. Gellhorn," she said. "The man who came to see you."

"What about him?"

I dreaded her answer.

"They found him dead," she said. "Imagine that. Just lying dead in a ditch."

"It might be a stranger altogether," I mumbled.

"Raymond J. Gellhorn," she said, sharply. "There can't be two, can there? The description fits, too. Lord, what a way to die! They found tire marks on his arms and body. Imagine! I'm glad it turned out to be a bus; otherwise they might have come poking around here."

"Did it happen near here?" I asked, anxiously.

"No... Near Cooksville. But, goodness, read about it yourself if you—What happened to Giuseppe?"

I welcomed the diversion. Giuseppe was waiting patiently for me to complete the repaint job. His windshield had been replaced.

After she left, I snatched up the transcript. There was no doubt about it. The doctor reported he had been running and was in a state of totally spent exhaustion. I wondered for how many miles the bus had played with him before the final lunge. The transcript had no notion of anything like that, of course.

They had located the bus and identified it by the tire tracks. The police had it and were trying to trace its ownership.

There was an editorial in the transcript about it. It had been the first traffic fatality in the state for that year, and the paper warned strenuously against manual driving after night.

There was no mention of Gellhorn's three thugs and for that, at least, I was grateful. None of our cars had been seduced by the pleasure of the chase into killing.

That was all. I let the paper drop. Gellhorn had been a criminal. His treatment of the bus had been brutal. There was no question in my mind he deserved death. But still I felt a bit queasy over the manner of it.

A month has passed now and I can't get it out of my mind. My cars talk to one another. I have no doubt about it anymore. It's as though they've gained confidence; as though they're not bothering to keep it secret anymore. Their engines rattle and knock continuously.

And they don't talk among themselves only. They talk to the cars and buses that come into the Farm on business. How long have they been doing that?

They must be understood, too. Gellhorn's bus understood them, for all it hadn't been on the grounds more than an hour. I can close my eyes and bring back that dash along the highway, with our cars flanking the bus on either side, clacking their motors at it till it understood, stopped, let me out, and ran off with Gellhorn.

Did my cars tell him to kill Gellhorn? Or was that his idea?

Can cars have such ideas? The motor designers say no. But they mean under ordinary conditions. Have they foreseen *everything?*

Cars get ill-used, you know.

Some of them enter the Farm and observe. They get told things. They find out that cars exist whose motors are never stopped, whom no one ever drives, whose every need is supplied.

Then maybe they go out and tell others. Maybe the word is spreading quickly. Maybe they're going to think that the Farm way should be the way all over the world. They don't understand. You couldn't expect them to understand about legacies and the whims of rich men.

There are millions of automatobiles on Earth, tens of millions. If the thought gets rooted in them that they're slaves; that they should do something about it... If they begin to think the way Gellhorn's bus did....

Maybe it won't be till after my time. And then they'll have to keep a few of us to take care of them, won't they? They wouldn't kill us all.

Or maybe they would. Maybe they wouldn't understand about how someone would have to care for them. Maybe they won't wait.

Every morning I wake up and think, Maybe today....

I don't get as much pleasure out of my cars as I used to. Lately, I notice that I'm even beginning to avoid Sally.

FULL CIRCLE

H. B. Hickey

Many people who study the history of science fiction believe that the first "real" sf novel was Mary Shelley's masterpiece, *Frankenstein*, first published in 1818. In this book, the author posed a question that has been at the heart of science fiction ever since—who will ultimately prevail, humankind or its creations? H. B. Hickey's story takes what Shelley began to perhaps its logical end—and then back to a new beginning?

"ATTENTION!"

From a thousand speakers, strategically placed, the voice came like a crash of thunder.

"Attention! Stop work!"

With a sound like earthquakes rumbling and mountains falling and the sweep of tidal waves, the machines ground to a halt. The vats ceased their bubbling and the tubes went dark.

In all the immensity of the factory, mile upon mile of sunlit vastness, there was no sound. A hundred feet high and a thousand feet long, machines reared up, waiting. In the vats, a million gallons to each, the liquids lay in flawless crimson sheets.

"An important announcement!" the voice thundered. "Final tests on the '63 model have been completed!"

Still silence, but now a waiting, wondering silence.

"Success!" the voice said. "Our fondest hopes have been exceeded!"

Pandemonium. Metal ringing on metal, multiplied a thousand, a million, a million million times, ringing and clashing and echoing until at last the echoes faded away.

"Yes," the voice said, and somewhat hushed now. "Success. In the year 20,362 we have achieved it.

"Without fear of exaggeration we may say that not since the dawn of time, not since that legendary and unrecorded day when we ourselves were created, has there been anything like the '63 model.

"You will soon have the complete story, but for the moment these few facts will suffice: the '63 model will require no servicing! It will run efficiently on almost any fuel available! It is self-repairing!

It will adjust automatically to an unbelievable range of temperature changes!"

Again pandemonium. And finally the voice again, rising above all other sounds.

"It is hardly necessary to add that production is high enough so that the '63 model will be available to all.

"And now—everything is ready, blueprints and materials are being fed to the machines. Back to work!"

In the factory the crimson liquids bubbled in the vats and surged through the pipes and were pierced by lightning bolts from the great vacuum tubes. Through the machines and the presses the solids flowed and were rolled and beaten and powdered. And there were all the gases necessary.

Oxygen and hydrogen and chlorine and cobalt and copper and iron and calcium and phosphorus and sodium and potassium; they combined and united and divided and were shattered and remade by millions of volts of artificial lightning.

And the machines roared and thundered and rumbled, and the sound was like the day of Creation.

And in Control there was no noise but equal activity. Here a green light indicated what a worker could not see, that Press X-B was rolling the surfacing too thin by a molecule layer. There an orange glow indicated a drop of a millionth of a degree in the temperature of Vat Q-9.

The words went out from Control. "Worker RR-7, up a millionth. Worker V-2, pressure up a micro-volt."

For nothing must go wrong. The '63 model must be perfection.

And in Distribution there was the clatter of smaller machines and the sound of words and words and words. The news must go out. Through all possible channels the news of the '63 model must be distributed.

Everyone must know so that everyone might be prepared.

AT LAST! MODEL '63!

SEE IT! HEAR IT! TEST IT!

NO HOME COMPLETE WITHOUT ONE!

So the news went out. For the first time, within the reach of all!

Perfection.

The '63 model. Perfection. The ultimate. Able to do anything and everything better than it had ever been done before. Perfection.

Self-servicing, self-fueling, self-directing!

Unbelievable, but true! No machine, no robot even, could do what the '63 model could do.

Out of the thunder of Production and the precision of Control and the Channels of Distribution the '63 model came. By the hundreds, the thousands, the millions, they poured out and were tested and lined up and carted away.

And to the showrooms of the world the robots came, in the year 20,362, to stand alone and in groups with their great metal bodies gleaming and their metallic voices hushed, to see the product of the Factory, the '63 model.

Unbelievable that skin so thin and soft could be so durable, that eyes so weak and watery could see so well, that a brain of such inferior materials could function.

But there it was, the '63 model, the Humanoid, and it postured and walked and talked, was truly everything it was claimed to be.

And the signs told the most unbelievable thing of all: that the '63 model could reproduce itself!

By the millions the robots came and saw and marveled at this thing that Robot had made. By the millions they took away with them the '63 model and wondered afresh at the genius of Robot.

But a few, seeing what Robot had created, felt a touch of fear.

TO AVENGE MAN

Lester Del Rey

This powerful, moving story by the distinguished science fiction writer and editor Les-
ter Del Rey asks one of the oldest questions
about our planet. Who will inherit the earth?
And if the answer is intelligent machines,
then what will those machines think of us?

I

Hate spewed across the galaxy in a high crusade. Metal ships leaped from world to world and hurtled across space to farther and farther stars. Planets surrendered their ores to sky-reaching cities, built around fortress temples and supported by vast networks of technology. Then more ships were spawned, armed with incredible weapons, and sent forth in the eternal search for an enemy.

In the teeming cities and aboard the questing ships, soul-wrenching music was composed, epic fiction and supernal poetry were written, and great paintings and sculpture were developed, to be forgotten as later and nobler work was done. Science strove for the ultimate limit of understanding, fought against that limit, and surged past it to limitless possibilities.

But behind all the arts and sciences lay the drive of religion. And the religion was one of ancient anger and dedicated hate.

The ships filled the galaxy until every world was conquered. For a time they hesitated, preparing for the great leap outward. Then the armadas sailed again, across thousands and millions of light-years toward the beckoning galaxies beyond.

With each ship went the holy image of their faith and the unsated and insatiable hunger of their hate...

II

The cat-track labored up the rough road over the crater wall, topped the last rise and began humming its way down into Aristarchus. As it dipped into the ink black of its own shadow from the sun behind, its headlights flashed on. Around it, the jagged rocky walls scintillated in a riot of reflected colors from crystal fractures that had never been dulled by wind or rain.

Inside the cab, the driver's seat groaned protestingly at the robot's weight as Sam shifted his six hundred terrestrial pounds forward. Coming home was always a good time. He switched lenses in his eyes and began scanning the crater floor for the first sight of the Lunar Base Dome, though he knew it was still hidden around a twist of the trail.

"You don't have to be quite so all-fired anxious to get back, Sam," Hal Norman complained. But the little selenologist was also gazing forward eagerly. "You might show some appreciation for the time I've spent answering your fool questions and trying to pound sense into your tin head. Anybody'd think you didn't like my company," he pouted humorously.

Sam made the sound of a human chuckle, as he had taught himself to acknowledge all the verbal nonsense men called humor. But truth compelled him to answer seriously. "I like your company very much, Hal."

He had always liked the company of the men he'd met on Earth or during his many years on the Moon. Humans, he had decided long ago, were wonderful. He had enjoyed the long field trip with Hal Norman while they collected data from the automatic recorders scattered over the lunar surface. But it would still be good to get back to the dome, where the men had given him the unique privilege of joining them. There he could listen to the often inexplicable but always fascinating conversation of forty men. And there, perhaps, he could join them in their singing.

Music and reading were the chief recreations of the men here. There were thousands of microbooks in the dome library, brought in a few at a time by many men over the long years. They were one of the few taboos. It was against orders for Sam to read any of them, and a man had once told him that it was to save him from unnecessary confusion. But the collection of music was not forbidden, and he was often permitted to join in their singing. All the robots had perfect pitch, of course. But only Sam had learned to sing acceptably enough to win a place in the dome.

In anticipation, he began humming a chanty about the sea he had never seen. The cat-track hummed downward between the walls of the road that had been crudely bulldozed from the rubble of the crater. Then they broke out into the open, and he could see the dome and the territory around it.

Hal grunted in surprise. "That's odd. I hoped the supply rocket would be in. But what are those three ships doing here?"

Sam cut off the headlights and switched back to wide-angle lenses. Now most of the crater was visible, until it vanished against the horizon, giving place to the blackness of the sky and the myriad colored pinpoints of the stars. Ahead lay the low dome that roofed the Base, with its biphase microwave antenna tracking the manned space platform that circled Earth. Half a mile beyond it stood three ships, bulky with exposed tanks and each carrying a huge passenger globe encased in bracing girders. They didn't look like supply rockets.

Sam's eyes swept across the crater floor, almost to the horizon. There he could make out the crumpled wreck of an early ship, still surrounded by the supply capsules that had been sent on automatic control to keep the stranded crew alive until rescue could be sent. The three ships bore a striking resemblance to the one that had crashed. The only other such ships were those used in the third expedition. But they had been parked in orbit around Earth after the end of the third expedition fifty years ago. Once the Base was established, their capacity had no longer been needed, and they were inefficient for routine supply shipment and the rotation of the men stationed here.

Before he could comment on the ships, the buzzer sounded, indicating that Base had spotted the cat-track. Sam flipped the switch and acknowledged the call.

"Hi, Sam." It was the voice of Dr. Robert Smithers, the leader of Lunar Base. "Butt out, will you? I want to talk to Hal."

Sam could have tuned in on the communication frequency with his own receptors, since the signal was strong enough at this distance. But he obeyed the order to avoid listening as Hal reached for the handset. There was no way to detune his audio receptors, however.

He heard Hal's greeting. Then there was silence for at least a minute.

Hal's face was shocked and serious when he finally spoke again. "But that's damned nonsense, Chief! Earth got over such insanity half a century ago. There hasn't been a sign of...Yes, sir...All right, sir. Thanks for not taking off without me."

He hung up the handset, shaking his head. When he faced Sam, his expression was unreadable. "Full speed, Sam."

"There's trouble," Sam guessed. He threw the cat-track into its top speed of thirty miles an hour, fighting and straining with the controls. Only a robot could manage the tricky machine at such a rate over the crude road, and it required his full attention.

Hal's voice was strange and harsh. "We're being sent back to Earth. Big trouble, Sam. But what can you know of war and rumors of war?"

"War was a dangerous form of political insanity, outlawed at the conference of 1983," Sam quoted from a speech that had come over the radio. "Human warfare has now become unthinkable."

"Yeah. Human war." Hal made a rough sound in his throat. "But not cruel and inhuman war, it seems...Oh, hell. Stop looking so gloomy; it's not your problem."

Sam decided against chuckling this time, though reference to his set, unsmiling expression was usually meant to be a form of humor. He filed the puzzling words away in his permanent memory for later consideration.

The terminator was rushing across the lunar surface. It would soon be night. More than half of the near crater was already hidden in blackness, though sunlight was still reaching the Base, and the territory beyond was in glaring white light. But the undiffused shadows stretched long behind every projection in the road. Seeing was hard as they neared the dome, and all Sam's attention had to be directed to his driving. Behind him, he heard Hal getting into the moonsuit to leave the cab.

Sam brought the cat-track to a halt to let Hal out at the entrance to the sealed underground hemisphere of lunar rock that was the true dome—the light upper structure was simply a shield against the heat of the sun. He drove the machine under that and shut off the motor.

As he emerged from the airlock, air gushed out of small cavities of his body and made a haze of glittering crystals that fell slowly to the surface. But he felt no discomfort. There was only the faint click as a pressure sensitive piezzo-electric switch activated a relay inside his torso. That switch was designed as an emergency measure, to turn his power on if there should be a puncture of the dome while he was inactivated, and now it merely indicated the pressure drop. Maybe one of the reasons the men liked having him inside was the existence of that switch, since it could save their lives—though he hoped there were other explanations. There had been no room in the Mark Three robots for such devices.

He saw some of the Mark Threes waiting just beyond the entrance as he approached. There were tracks in the lunar dust leading to the space ships, but whatever ferrying they had done was obviously finished, and they were merely standing in readiness. They were totally unlike him.

Sam bulked over the tiny black robots. One of them, directly in his path, slipped under his raised arm to make room for him, moving with a light gracefulness that he couldn't approximate. He was bulky and mechanical, designed only for function, in the early days when men needed help on the Moon. The Mark Threes were almost childlike, under their dark enamel, and their size and weight had been pared down to less than that of a man. There had been thirty of the model originally, but accidents had left only a few more than twenty. And of the original Mark Ones, only Sam was still functioning.

"When do we leave?" he called to one of the little robots over the radio circuit.

The black head turned slowly toward him. "We do not know. The men did not tell us."

"Didn't you ask them?" he called. But he had no need of their denial. They had not been told to ask.

They were still unformed, less than five years old, and their thoughts were tied to the education given by the computers in the creche. They lacked more than twenty years of his intimate association with men. But sometimes he wondered whether they would ever learn enough, or whether they had been too strongly repressed in training. Men were afraid of robots back on Earth, as Hal Norman had once told him, which was why they were still being used only on the Moon.

He turned away from them and went down the entrance to the inner dome. The entrance led to the great community room, and the men were all gathered there, wearing moonsuits. They were arguing with Hal as he began emerging from the lock, but at sight of Sam the words were cut off. He stared about in the silence, feeling suddenly awkward.

"Hello, Sam," Dr. Smithers said finally. He was a tall, spare man barely thirty, but seven years of responsibility here had etched deep lines into his face and put gray in his mustache, though his other hair was still jet black. "All right, Hal. Your things are on the ship. I cut it fine waiting for you, so we're leaving at once. No more arguments. Get out there!"

"Go to hell!" Hal told him. "I don't desert my friends."

Other men began moving out. Sam stepped aside to let them pass, but they seemed to avoid looking at him.

Smithers sighed wearily. "Hal, I can't argue this with you. You'll go if I have to chain you. Do you think I like this? But we're under military orders now. They're going crazy back there. They didn't find out about the expected attack until a week ago, as near as I can learn, but they've already canceled space. Damn it, I can't take him! We're at the ragged limit of available lift now, and he represents six hundred pounds of mass—more than four of the others," he raised his arms slightly.

Hal gestured sharply toward the outside. "Then leave four of *those* behind. He's worth more than the whole lot of them."

"Yeah. He is. But my orders specify that all men and the maximum possible number of robots must be returned." Smithers twisted his lips savagely and suddenly turned to face the robot. "Sam, I'll give it to you straight. I can't take you with us. We have to leave you here alone. I'm sorry, but that's how it has to be."

"You won't be alone, Sam," Hal Norman said. "I'm staying."

Sam stood silently for a moment, letting it register. His circuits found it hard to integrate. He had never thought of being separated from these men who had been his life. Going back to Earth had been easy to accept; he'd gone back there once before. Little hopes and future-pictures he hadn't known were in his mind began to appear.

But with those came memories of Hal Norman's expressed hopes and dreams. The man had showed Sam a picture of his future wife and tried to describe all that such a creature meant to a man. He'd spoken of green fields and the sea. He'd raved about Earth too often during the days they were together.

Sam moved forward toward Hal. The man saw him coming

and began to back away, but he was no match for the robot. Sam held his arms and closed the moonsuit, then gathered the man up carefully. Hal was struggling, but it did no good against Sam's determination.

"All right, Dr. Smithers. We can go now," Sam told the Chief.

They were the last to leave the dome. The little black robots were already marching across the surface, with the men straggling along behind them. Smithers fell into step with Sam, moving as if the burden was on his back instead of in the arms of the robot. Hal had ceased struggling. He lay outwardly quiet; but through the suit, Sam's body receptors picked up sounds that he had heard only twice before on occasions he tried not to remember. They were the sounds of a man trying to control his weeping.

Halfway to the ships, faint words came over the radio. "Put me down, Sam. I'll go quietly."

Sam obeyed, and the three moved on together. Smithers' hand touched Sam's shoulder, and the man's words came through his suit. "Thanks, Sam. Handling Hal was a favor I no longer had the right to ask of you. Well, it looks as if you're going to have a lot of time to kill. And we..."

He didn't finish the thought. Sam mulled over the words he could understand, and even they made no sense. With the men all gone, there would be no spare time. There would be more than he could possibly find time to accomplish. The great solar observatory across the crater would need tending, the selenographs would have to be checked and at least the routine reports from all instruments would have to be sent off weekly. He should have had hours of instructions, but now it looked as if there would be no time for more than hasty orders.

By the time the three reached the nearest ship, the other men and the little robots were all aboard. The Chief motioned Hal up the ramp. For a moment the younger man hesitated. He turned toward Sam, started to make a motion, and then swung away and dashed into the ship, his shoulders shaking convulsively.

Smithers still stood after the others had disappeared. The radio brought the sound of a sigh, before the man moved. But there were no words.

"You haven't given me my orders," Sam reminded him.

Smithers shook his head, as if coming out of some deeper thoughts of his own. His lips twitched into what might have been a smile. "No, Sam. There are no orders. All orders, past, present or future—all are canceled. There is no more work. Space is finished!"

He put his foot on the ramp and turned partly away from Sam. Then abruptly he swung back.

"Good-by, Sam," he said thickly. His right hand lifted in a brief gesture. "Don't forget the books!"

A moment later, he was through the entrance to the ship. The ramp was drawn in after him, and the great outer seal of the rocket ship began to close.

III

Sam ran back to the entrance to the dome, to avoid the blast. As he ran, he realized slowly the meaning of what Smithers had said.

No orders! There hadn't even been orders left for him to come back here, back to the place men had left. Yet his feet went on moving, as if acting on some strange orders of their own.

The edge of darkness had touched the dome now, leaving the rocket standing in the last light as he turned back. He watched the takeoff of the three heavily laden ships. They staggered up slowly on great tails of flame. They rose on sharper jets until they were above the crater walls and against the black of space, carrying the men toward the rendezvous with Earth's orbital station. Sam watched until they were beyond the range of his strongest vision. Then, without orders or knowledge of why he acted, he turned into the dome. It was silent and empty around him.

He stared at the clock on the wall and at the calendar that they had kept marked off. He hadn't found out how long they would be gone. But Smithers' words gave a vague answer—he would have a lot of time to kill. That could mean anywhere from one month to most of a year, judging by the application of similar phrases in the past. He looked at the shelves filled with microbooks for a few moments. Then he went outside, to stare up at the Earth in the sky above him. There were spots of light in the dark areas that he knew to be the cities of men. There were men there, a quarter of a million miles away, and there must be speech and man-laughter and singing.

He stood there a long time, staring upwards. Finally he went back inside, to tidy up the mess the men had made in their hasty leaving. He folded the few spare clothes and put them away, cleaned the cooking equipment and straightened up as best he could. Hal had left the picture of the female man about whom he'd spoken so often, and Sam stared at it, trying again to understand. At last, he put it carefully into a drawer, closing it away from view.

The microbooks Hal had liked to keep near him were in the same drawer, and they reminded Sam of Smithers' last words.

"Don't forget the books!" The words seemed needless, since Sam could never forget unless ordered to do so. And the Chief had said there were no orders. There wasn't even an order against reading the books now.

And that, Sam realized, might have been what Smithers was indicating to him in those final words.

The second day after the takeoff of the ship, Sam was watching the dark areas of Earth again when some of them grew suddenly brighter. New spots of brightness rose and decayed during the hours he watched. They were far brighter than any city should have been. Other spots glowed where no cities had been before. But eventually, they all faded. After that, there were no bright areas at all.

As Earth turned slowly, he saw that all the cities on Earth were now dark.

It was a mystery for which he had no explanation. He went inside to try the radio that brought news and entertainment from the relay on the orbital station, but no signal was coming through. He debated calling them, but initiating such a call was reserved for Smithers. And he was gone.

He was outside again, staring at Earth the next time the familiar spots that should have been cities swam into the darkened side of Earth. There were still no spots of lights. Even with the small telescope used for the infrequent observations of Earth, he could detect no sign of the cities. There was only the hint of a dull glow in a few places, too diffuse to be from normal lights. And the radio was silent.

He paced about, trying to force his eyes to see what was not there to see. Men had to be there! And the lights of their cities would be the proof of it—the assurance that men were still talking and making what they called jokes and singing, even if they were beyond his hearing. Now suddenly, he needed that proof, and there was no evidence! It was as if all men had disappeared with the going of the few from the Moon!

Through all the fifth day, he waited before the radio with the gain turned up to its maximum. The men who had left here should have arrived at their destination now. He knew there was no reason to expect such a call; men were not obligated to report to a robot, as they would have reported to other men. But his brain circuits had been filled with odd future-pictures that drove him to the set and kept him there for long hours after he knew there would be no signal for him.

Finally, he knew there would be no call. He got up and went into the empty room where the men had spent so much of their time.

Eventually his pacing led him to the music player. They had let him use it at times, and he turned to it now, to fill the emptiness of the room and of his mind with sound. He found a tape that was one of his favorites and threaded it. But when the final chorus of Beethoven's Ninth reached its end, the dome seemed more empty and silent than ever. He found another tape, without voices this time. And that was followed by another. It helped a little, but it was not enough.

It was then that he turned to the books, taking one at random. It was something about Mars, by a human named Edgar Rice Burroughs, and he started to put it back. He had already learned enough about astronomy from the education machine. But at last he threaded it into the microreader and sat down to read.

It started well enough, and it was about some strange kind of man, not about astronomy. But then...

Sam made a strange sound, only slowly realizing that he had imitated the groan of a man for the first time in his existence. It was all madness!

He knew men had never reached Mars—and couldn't reach *this* Mars, because the planet was totally unlike what he knew existed. It must be some strange form of human humor. Or else there were men unlike any he had known and facts that had been kept from him. The latter seemed more probable.

He struggled through it, to groan again when it ended and

he still didn't know what had happened to the strange female man who was a princess and who laid highly impossible eggs. But by then he had begun to like John Carter. He wanted to read more. He was confused—but even more curious than puzzled. Eventually, he found the whole series and read them all.

It was much later that one of the books solved some of the puzzle for him. There was a small note before the book really began: *This is a work of speculative fiction; any resemblance to present-day persons or events is entirely coincidental.* He looked up *fiction* in the dictionary he had seen the men use and felt better afterwards. It wasn't quite like humor, but it wasn't fact, either. It was a game of some kind, where the rules of life were all changed about in idiosyncratic ways. The writer might pretend that men liked to kill each other or were afraid of women, or some other ridiculous idea; then he tried to show what might happen. It was obviously taboo to pretend about real people and events, though some of the books had stories that used names and backgrounds that had the same names as those in reality.

The best fiction of all sometimes looked like books of fact, if the writer was clever enough. "History" was mostly that. There was a whole imaginary world called Rome, for instance. It was fortunate that Sam had been taught the simple facts of man's progress by the education machine before reading such books. Men, it was true, had sometimes been violent, but not when they understood all the facts or could help it.

In the end he evolved a simple classification. If a book made him think hard and forced him to strain to follow it, it was fact; if it made him read faster and think less as he went through it, it was fiction.

There was one book that was hardest of all to classify. It was an old book, written before men had gone out into space. Yet it was full of carefully documented and related facts about an invasion of flying saucers from far in space. Eventually he was forced to decide from the internal evidence that it was fact; but it left him disturbed and unhappy.

Hal Norman had referred to inhuman war, and Dr. Smithers had mentioned an attack. Could it be that the strange ships from somewhere had struck Earth?

He remembered the brilliant lights over the cities, so much like the great ray weapons described in some of the fiction about space war. Sometimes there were elements of truth even in fiction. There had been a book about men who went back in time and fought totally impossible monsters—and then he had discovered that there really had been dinosaurs of that size and kind.

There was a book about those who spoke for Boskone, and puzzling suggestions that the evil men who seemed to have existed were agents of the Boskone, or of the Eich. It would at least explain why the probably fictional Hitler could be treated as fact, in books that otherwise did not seem to be fiction.

If invaders had come in great ships to fight against Earth, it might take men longer than Sam cared to think about to fight them off. If there were flying saucers or ships of the Eich attacking Earth, some of his men might never come back at all! And there was nothing Sam could do here to help them.

He went outside to stare at the sky. Earth still showed no sign of cities. They must be blacked out, as they would be if flying saucers were in their skies. He searched the space over the Moon, but he could find no strange craft. Then he went back inside to read through the microbooks again.

It was poetry that somehow finally shoved the worry from his mind. He had tried poetry before, and given up, unable to follow it. But this time he made a discovery. He tried reading it aloud, until it began to beat at him and force its rhythm on him. He was reading Swinburne's *Hymn of Man,* attracted by the title, and suddenly the words and something besides began to sing their way into his deepest mind.

He went back over four lines again and again, until they were music, or all that music had tried to say and had failed:

"In the grey beginning of years, in the
twilight of things that began,
The word of the earth in the ears of
the world, was it God? was it man?"

Sam went up and down the dome for most of that day, chanting to himself that the word of the earth in the ears of the world was *man!* Then he turned back to other poetry.

None quite equaled that one experience, but most of it stirred his circuits in strange ways. A book of limericks even surprised him twice to the point where he chuckled, without realizing that he had never done that spontaneously before.

There were slightly over four thousand volumes in the little library, including the technical books. He timed them carefully, stretching them by rereading his favorites, until he finished the last at exactly midnight on the eve of the takeoff anniversary.

The next twenty-four hours he spent outside the dome, watching the sky and staring at Earth, while his radio receptors scanned all the frequencies.

It had been a lot of time already killed. But there was no signal, and no rocket ship blasted down, bringing back the men.

At midnight he gave a sighing sound and went back inside the dome. In the technical section, he unlocked the controls for the atomic generator and turned it down to its lowest idling rate. He came back, turning the now dim lights off as he moved. In the main room, he put his favorite tape on the player and the copy of Swinburne in the microreader. But he did not turn them on. Instead, he dropped his heavy body quietly onto the floor before the entrance, where the men would be sure to see him when they finally returned.

Then one hand reached up firmly, and he turned himself off.

IV

Sam's eyes turned toward the entrance as consciousness snapped on again. There was no sign of men there. He stood up, staring about the dome, then hastened outside to stare across the floor of the crater. It lay bare, except for the old wrecked rocket ship.

Men had not come back.

Inside again, he looked for something that might have fallen and hit his switch. The switch itself was still in the off position, however. And when he turned on the tape player, no sound came. It was confirmation enough. Something had happened to the air in the dome, and his internal switch had gone into operation to turn him on automatically.

A few minutes later he found the hole. A meteoroid the size of an egg must have hit the surface above. It had struck with enough force to blast a tiny craterlet almost completely through the dome, and internal pressure had done the rest.

He secured patching material and began automatically making the repairs. There was still more than enough air in the tanks to fill the dome again.

Sam sighed as the first whisper of sound reached him from the tape player. He flipped his switch back to the on position before the rising pressure negated the emergency circuit. He still had to get back to the entrance to resume his vigil. It had simply been bad luck that had aroused him before the men could return.

He moved back through the dome, hardly looking. But his eyes were open, and his mind gradually began to add the evidence. There was no way to tell how long he had been unconscious; he had no feeling of any time. But there was dust over everything—dust that had been disturbed by the outrushing air, but that had still patina-plated itself on metal firmly enough to remain. And some of the metal showed traces of corrosion. That must have taken years!

He stopped abruptly, checking his battery power. The cobalt-platinum cell had been fully charged when he lay down. Now it was at less than half charge. Such batteries had an extremely slow leakage. Even allowing for residual conductance through his circuits, it would have taken at least thirty years for such a loss!

Thirty years! And the men had not come back.

A groan came to his ears, and he turned quickly. But it had only been his own voice. And now he began shouting. He was still trying to shout in the airless void as he reached the surface. He caught himself, bracing his back against the dome as his balance circuits reacted to some wild impulse from his brain.

Men would never desert him. They had to come back to the Moon to finish their work, and the first thing they would do would be to find him. Men couldn't just leave him there! Only in the wild fiction could that happen, and even there only the postulated evil men would do such a thing. *His* men would never dream of it!

He stared up at Earth. The dome was in night again, and Earth was a great orb in the sky, glowing blue and white, with touches of brown in a few places. He saw the outline of continents through the cloud cover, and recognized the great cities that must lie within the thin darkened area. There should have been lights visible there, even against the contrast of brighter Earthlight.

But there was no light.

He sighed soundlessly again, and now he felt himself relaxing. The attackers must still be hovering there! The dangerous Ufo-things from space. Men were still embattled and unable to return to him. Thirty years of that for them, and here he was losing balance over what had been only a year of his conscious time!

He faced the worst of possibilities more calmly now. He even forced himself to admit that men might have been so badly crippled by the war that they could not return to him—perhaps not for more time than he could think of. Smithers had said they were abandoning space, at a time when the attack had not yet come. How long would it take to recover and regain their lost territory?

He went back into the dome, but the radio was silent. Hesitantly, he initiated a call to the orbital station. After half an hour, he gave up. The men there, if men were still there, must be keeping strict radio silence.

"All right," he said slowly into the silence of the dome. "All right, face it. Men aren't coming back for a robot. Ever!"

It was a speech out of the fiction he had read, rather than out of rationality. But somehow saying it loudly made it easier to face. Men could not come to him. He wasn't that valuable to them.

He shook his head over that, remembering the time he had been taken back to Earth after twenty years out of the creche and on the Moon. The Mark One robots were sent to replace them, but they had been beset by some circuit flaws that made them more prone to accident and less useful than the first models. More than a hundred had been sent in all—and none had remained. It was then they called Sam back to study him.

There, deep in the security-hidden underground robot development workshops, he had been tested in every way they knew to help them in designing the Mark Three robots. And there old Stephen DeMatre had interviewed him for three whole days. At the end of that time, the man who·had first introduced him to his place with men put a hand on his metal shoulder and smiled at him.

"You're unique, Sam," he'd said. "A lucky combination of all the wild guesses we used in making each Mark One individually, as well as some unique conditioning among that first Base staff. We don't dare duplicate you yet, but some day the circuit control computer is going to want to get your pattern in full for later brains. So take good care of yourself. I'd keep you here, but...You take care of yourself, Sam. You hear me?"

Sam had nodded. "Yes, sir. Do you mean you can make other brains exactly like mine?"

"Technically, the control computer can duplicate your design," DeMatre had answered. "It won't be just like your brain— too many random factors in any really advanced mechanical mind unit—but with similar capabilities. That's why you're worth quite a few million dollars, and it's up to you to see valuable property like that isn't destroyed. Right, Sam?"

Sam had agreed and been shipped back to the Moon, along with the first of the Mark Three robots. And maybe his trip back had been of some use, since the new models worked as well as their limitations permitted. They were far better than the preceding models.

Maybe he wasn't valuable enough to men for them to come for him now. But by DeMatre's own words, he was one of their most valuable possessions. If it was up to him to see that he wasn't destroyed, then it was up to him also to see that he wasn't lost to men.

If they couldn't come for him, he had to go to them.

The question was: How? He couldn't project himself by mind power like John Carter. He had to have a rocket!

With the thought, he went dashing out through the entrance and heading toward the old wreck. It stood exactly as it had after the landing that had ruined it, with half its hull plating ripped off and most of its rocket motors broken. It could never be flown again. Nor could the old supply capsules. They had burned out their tubes in getting here, being of minimum construction. There wasn't even room inside one for him.

Sam considered it, making measurements and doing the hardest thinking of his existence. Without the long study of all the technical manuals of the dome library, he could never have found an answer. But eventually he nodded.

A motor from the big shop could be fitted to a capsule. It would be barely strong enough. But the plating could be removed to lighten the little ship; Sam needed no protection from space.

And the automatic guidance system could be removed to make enough room for him. He could operate it manually, since his reaction and integrating times were faster than that of even the system.

Fuel would be a problem, though there was enough oxygen in the dome storage tanks. It would have to be hydrogen, since he could find rocks from which that could be released by the power of the generator. Fortunately, lunar gravity was easier to escape than that of Earth.

He went back to the dome and found paper and pencil. He was humming softly to himself as he began laying out his plan. It wasn't easy. He might not be skilled enough to pilot the strange craft to the station. And it would take a great deal of time. But Sam was going to the men who wouldn't come to him!

V

It takes experience to turn engineering theory into practice. Almost three years had passed since Sam's awakening before the orbital station swam slowly into view before him. And the erratic takeoff and flight had been one that no human body could have stood. But now he sighted on the huge metal doughnut before him, estimating its orbit carefully. There were only a few gallons of fuel remaining in the tanks behind him, and he had to reach the landing net at the first try.

His first calculations seemed wrong. He glanced down at the huge orb of Earth and flipped sun filters over his eyes. Something was wrong. The station was not holding its bottom pointed exactly at the center of the Earth as it should have done; it was turning very slowly, and even its spin was uneven, as if the water used to balance it against wobbling had not been distributed properly. Beside it, the little ferry ship used between station and ships from Earth was jerking slightly on the silicone-plastic line that held it.

Sam felt an unpleasant stirring in his chest where most of his brain circuits lay. But he forced it down and computed his blast for all the factors. He had learned something of the behavior of his capsule during the minutes of takeoff and the later approach to the station. His fingers moved delicately, and fuel metered out to the cranky little motor.

It was not a perfect match, but he managed to catch himself in the net around the entrance to the hub. He pulled himself free, as the capsule drifted off, and began scrambling up to the lock. A moment later, he was standing in the weightlessness of the receiving section. And from the sounds of his feet, there was still air in the station.

He froze motionless as he let himself realize he had made it. Then he began looking for the men who should have seen his approach and be coming to question him.

There was no sound of steps or of any other activity, except for his own movements. Nor was there any light from the bulbs above him. The only illumination was from a thick quartz port that faced directly into the sun.

Sam cut on the lamp built into his chest, and began sweeping the sections of the hub with its light. Dust had formed a patina here, too. He sighed softly into the air. Then he moved toward the outer sections, his step determined.

Halfway down the tube that ran from the hub to the outer hull, Sam stopped and cut off his light. Ahead of him there was a glow! Lights were still burning!

He let out a yell to call the men and began running, adjusting for the increasing feeling of weight as he moved outward. Then he was under the bulb.

He stared up at it—a single bulb burning among several others that were black, though they were on the same circuit. How long did it take for these bulbs to burn out? Years surely, and probably decades. Yet most of the station was in darkness, though there was still power from the atomic generator.

He found a few other bulbs burning in the outer station, but not many. The great reception and recreation room was empty. Beyond that, the offices were mostly open and vacant. Some held a litter of paper and other stuff, as if someone had gone through carelessly, not bothering to put anything back in place. The living section with its tiny sleeping cubicles was worse. Some of the rooms were simply bare, but others were in complete disorder. Four showed signs of long occupancy, with the sleeping nets worn almost through and not replaced. But nothing showed how recently they had been left.

He went through another section devoted to station machinery and came to a big room that was apparently now used for storage. Sam had seen a plan of the station in one of the older books in the dome. He placed this room as one designed as a storage for hydrogen bombs once. But that had been from the pre-civilized days of men, and the bombs had been dismantled and destroyed more than sixty years before.

It was in the hydroponics room that he was forced to face the truth. The plants there had been the means of replacing the oxygen in the air for the men, and now the tanks were dry and the vegetation had been dead so long that only dessicated stalks remained. There could be no men here. He didn't need the sight of the bare food section for confirmation. Some men had stayed here until the food was gone before they left the untended plants to die. It must have been many years ago that they had abandoned the station.

Sam shook his head in anger at himself. He should have guessed it when he saw that there were none of the winged rocket ships waiting outside the station. So long as men were here, they would have kept some means for return to Earth.

The observatory was dark, but there was still power for the electronic telescope. The screen lighted at his touch, showing only empty space. He had to wait nearly two hours before the slow tumble of the station brought Earth into full view.

Most of it was in daylight, and there was only a thin cloud cover. Once a thousand cities could have been scanned plainly from here. When seeing was best, even streams of moving cars could be seen. But now there were no cities and no signs of movement!

Sam emitted a harsh gasping sound as he scanned the continent of North America. He had seen pictures of New York, Chicago and several other city complexes from this view. Now there was only dark ruin showing where they had been. It came to him with an almost physical shock that perhaps millions of human beings had died in those wrecks of cities.

There were still smaller towns where he could make out the pattern of houses. But there was no movement, even there.

He cut power from the telescope with an angry flick of his finger, trying to blot the things he had seen from his memory. A moment later, he had power on again and was hunting down roadways and rivers for signs of movement. But there was no evidence of man. And all of the ruins looked old and weathered, as if there had been no man to fight on for a great many years.

He sagged against the telescope, his mind filled with pictures he could not control. Great ships ravening out of space, carrying savage alien monsters and bringing planet-wrecking rays against Earth. There had been no Lens, no miracle to save Earth. There had been only the ruin of all man's achievements. And man had been gone before Sam had finished his first year of waiting.

He shook off his imaginings by force of will. There had been men here on the station. They must have left some records.

He moved rapidly away from the observatory, hunting for the communications section. It was in worse shape than most other places when he found it. It looked as if some man had deliberately tried to wreck the machinery. A hammer lay tangled in a maze of ruin that must once have been the main receiver. There was something that looked like dried blood on a metal cabinet, with a dent that might have fitted a human fist.

The floor was littered with tape that should have held a record of all the communications received and sent, and the drive capstan on the tape player was bent into uselessness. Sam lifted a section of tape and placed it in the slot that gave his face a sad caricature of a mouth. The tape sensors moved into place, and he began scanning the bit of plastic. It was blank, probably wiped of any message by time and the unshielded transformer that was still humming below the control panel.

Most of the tape cabinet was empty, and there was nothing on tapes within. Sam ripped open drawers, hunting for some evidence. He finally found a single tape in the cabinet dented by a fistprint, lying at the back with the reel broken as if it had been hurled savagely into the drawer. Most of the impression on the tape was a garble of static; stray fields had gotten to it, even through the metal of the cabinet. But towards the end, a few words could barely be picked out from the noise.

"...test chambers here away from the blast...Thought we'd made it...a starving...went mad. Must have been a nerve aerosol, but it didn't settle as...Mad. Everywhere. Southern hemisphere, too. Your men who came down here didn't have a chance...Took a chance after I heard your broadcasts, but finding

a transmitter was diffi...Weeks. Now I'm the last survivor. I must
be. For God's sake, stay where you are! Don't..."

The noise grew worse then, totally ruining intelligibility. Sam
caught bits of what might have been sentences, but they made
no sense to him; they seemed to be pure gibberish. Then suddenly
a small section of the tape against the hub became almost clear.

The voice was high-pitched now, and overmodulated, as if
the words had been too loud to be carried by the transmitter.
There was a strange, unpleasant quality that Sam had never heard
in a human voice before.

"...all shiny and bright. But it couldn't fool me. I knew it was
one of them! They're waiting up there, waiting for me to come out.
They want to eat my soul. They're clever now, they won't let me
see them. But when I turn back, I can feel..."

The tape came to an end.

Sam could make no sense of it, though he replayed it all
again in hopes of finding some other clue. He gave up and reached
down to shut off the power in the transformer. It was amazing that
the wreckage hadn't already blown all the fuses for this section.
He groped for the switch and flipped it, just as his eyes spotted
something under the transformer shelf.

It was a fountain pen, gold and black enamel.

Sam had seen one like it countless times, and now he turned
it over in his hands, to see familiar lettering engraved on the barrel:
RPS. Those were the initials of Dr. Smithers, and the pen could
only have been his. He'd been one of those who had reached the
station, probably one who had waited there to receive that strange
message from Earth. The Moon ships had made it safely, and
Smithers had stayed on here until the food was gone. Then he
must have returned to Earth where the tape indicated at least one
man still survived, after the attack was over.

The telescope had showed no sign of men. But if there were
only a few men left on the immense face of the planet below, the
chance of finding any evidence of them was too slight to determine.

The search must be made from the surface of Earth, not
from this useless station in the sky.

In theory, getting back to Earth from the station wasn't too
difficult. A small retro-thrust from a rocket could slow its speed
and change its orbit enough to bring it down to the atmosphere.

Then any winged craft with shallow enough an angle of glide could be maneuvered down slowly to avoid burning from the friction of the air.

There was more than enough sheet metal in the sheathing of the station to provide modifications to the little ferry, and there were books that showed most details of the design of the regular landing craft. There was even enough fuel; the emergency tanks in the stations were half filled with the monopropellant suited for the little rocket motor in the ferry.

Sam had allowed himself perhaps a month to complete the task. But at the end of that time, he was swearing, using unprofane but colorful words he had learned from a score of historical novels. By then he was beginning to realize that the gap between theory and practice was enormous. He would be lucky to finish his work in a year, and then the results would be crude and uncertain.

The sheet metal was already all work-hardened, and there was no annealing oven to prepare it for reshaping. There was no press or large sheet metal brake in the tiny shop provided in the station. Even the welders were designed only for small repair. No transformer was suitable for constructing a larger welder, and he was forced to rewind one of the power cores, hoping that it would carry the amperage he needed.

It took two weeks of hard work to draw in the ferry, tie it down firmly to the hub against the wobbling of the station, and construct a crude scaffolding around it. Then he discovered that the hub was in the shadow of the station too much of the time, making metal there brittle with cold. The whole job had to be undone, the ferry moved to the top of the station and the entire scaffolding rebuilt.

The framework for his wings, controls and nose cone had to be built up by welding together a network of small plumbing pipes; they were too heavy and he was forced to build another framework through the walls of the ferry and across most of the small cabin. It left him barely room for himself. Then he discovered by bitter trial that there was no way to form the sheet metal around the frame without so much welding that air turbulence would have made atmospheric maneuvering quite impossible.

He finally was forced to hand form his wing covering on a crude mold built on the main deck of the station, fighting to force the sheets into their proper curves by repeated careful hammering.

When finally finished, they were too large to move through the halls, and he was forced to cut a new path out through the station. It was made possible only because he had no need of air to breathe.

Even the fuel turned out to be a problem. Thirty years of sitting in the tanks had started a slow process that resulted in small tarry filaments throughout. Pint by slow pint, it had to be filtered and refiltered until it was clear enough to pass through the tiny nozzle of the injector on the motor. By then he knew it would have been simpler to centrifuge it. But at last it was done.

VI

Surprisingly, the modified ferry behaved far better than Sam had dared to hope. It heated badly at the first touches of atmosphere, but the temperature remained within the limits he and the craft could stand. He learned slowly to control the descent to a glide neither too shallow for stability nor too steep to avoid overheating. By the time he was down to thirty miles above the surface, he was almost pleased with the way it handled.

He had set his course to reach the underground creche that had been his home at awakening and during the first three years of his education, before they sent him to the Moon. It was the only home he knew on Earth.

Now he saw that he could never make it. The first fifteen minutes in the upper layers of atmosphere had been at too steep a glide angle, and he could never reach far inland. He might even have trouble reaching the shore at all, he realized; when the clouds thinned, he could see nothing but ocean under him.

He opened the rocket motor behind him gently, letting its thrust raise his speed to the highest his little craft could take at this altitude. But there was too little fuel left to help much. It might have given him an extra twenty miles of glide, but no more.

Sam considered the prospects of landing in the water with grim foreboding. He could exist in it for a while, even at fair depths. If he landed near the shore, he might work his way out. But within a limited period of time, the water would penetrate through his body to some of the vital wiring. Once that was shorted, he would cease to exist.

He came down under the clouds, fighting for every inch of altitude. Then, far ahead, he could see the shore. There were no islands here, so it had to be the mainland. Once there, he could reach the creche in a single day.

He passed over the shoreline at a height of five hundred feet. There was a short stretch of sand, some woods, and then a long expanse of green that must be grass. He eased the control forward, then back again.

The little ship came skimming down at two hundred miles an hour. Its skids touched the surface, and it bounced upwards. Sam fought the controls to keep it from nosing over. Again it touched, jerking with deceleration. This time it seemed to have struck right. Then a hummock of ground caught against one skid. The craft slithered sideways and flipped over. Sam braced himself as the ship began coming to pieces around him.

He pulled himself out, staring at the wreckage. It was a shame that it was ruined, he thought. But it couldn't be made as strong as he was and still glide through the air.

He turned to study the world around him. The grass was knee-high, moving gently in the wind. Beyond it lay woods. Sam had seen only pictures of trees like that before. He moved toward them, noticing the thickness of the underbrush around them. Below them, the dirt was dark and moist. He lifted a pinch to his face, moving his smell receptors forward in his mouth slit. It was a rich smell, richer than the stuff in the hydroponic tanks. He lifted his head to look for the birds he expected, but he could see no sign of them. There were only insects, buzzing and humming.

The sun had already set, he noticed. Yet it was not yet dark. There was a paling of the light, and a soft diffusion. He shook his head. Above him, tiny twinkling spots began to appear. He had read that stars twinkled, but he had thought it only fiction. He had never been under the open sky of Earth before.

Then a soft murmur of sound reached him. He started away, to be drawn back to it. Slowly he realized it was a sound like the description of that heard near the sea. He had never seen an ocean, either. And now one lay no more than a mile away.

He stumbled through the woods in the growing darkness. For some reason, he was reluctant to turn on his light. Eventually he learned to make his way through the brush and around the trees. The sound grew louder as he progressed.

It was dark when he reached the seashore, but there was a hint of faint light to the east. As he watched, it increased. A pale white arc appeared over the horizon and grew to a large circle. The Moon, he realized finally.

The waves rose and fell, booming into surf. And far out across the sea, the Moon seemed to ride on the waves, casting a silver road of light over the water.

Sam had read the word. Now for the first time, he found an understanding of it. This was Beauty.

He sighed as he heaved himself from the sand and began heading along the shore in search of a road that would take him westward. No wonder men wanted to come back to defend a world where something like this could be seen.

The Moon rose higher as he moved on, its light now bright enough to give him clear vision. He came over a small rise in the ground and spotted what seemed to be a road beyond it. Beside the road was a house. It was dark and quiet, but he swung aside, going through a copse of woods to reach it and search for any evidence of humanity.

The windows were mostly broken he saw as he approached. And weeds had grown up around it. There was a detached building beside it that held a small car, by what he could see through the single dusty window. He skirted that and reached the door of the house; it opened at his touch, its hinges protesting rustily.

Inside, the moonlight shone through the broken windows on a jumble of furniture that was overturned and scattered in no order Sam could see. And there were other things—white things that lay sprawled about on the floor.

He recognized them from the pictures in the books—skeletons of human beings. Two small skeletons were tangled in one corner with their skulls bashed in. A male skeleton lay near them, with the rusty shape of a knife shoved through a scrap of clothing between two ribs. There was a revolver near one hand. Across the room, a female skeleton was a jumbled pile of bones, with a small hole in the skull that could have come from a bullet.

Sam backed out of the room. He knew the meaning of another word now. He had seen Madness.

Men had learned to build good machines. The car motor barely turned over after Sam had figured out the controls, but it caught and began running with only a slight sputtering. The tires were slightly soft, but they took the bumps of the rutted little rail. Later, when Sam found a better road, they lasted under the punishment of high speed. Most of the road was clear. There were few vehicles along its way, and most of those seemed to have drifted to the shoulder before they stopped or crashed.

The sun was just rising when Sam located the place where the factory and warehouse had served as a legitimate cover for the secret underground robot project. Fire and weather had left only gutted ruins and rusty things that had once been machines. But the section that housed the creche entrance now stood apart from the rest, almost unharmed.

Sam moved into it and to the metal door openly concealed among other such doors. He should probably not have known the combination, but men were often careless among robots. He had been curious enough to note the details, and Sam did not forget. He bent to what seemed to be an ornamental grille and called out a series of numbers.

The door seemed to stick a little, but then it moved aside. Beyond lay the elevator, and that operated smoothly at the combination he punched. Power was still on, at least. There was no light, but the bulbs sprang into life as he found a switch.

He called out once, but he no longer expected to find men so easily. The place had the feel of abandonment. And while it could have protected its workers from almost anything, there had been only enough food and water stocked here for two weeks. There were a few signs that it had been used for a shelter, but most of it was still in very good order.

He moved past offices and laboratories toward the back. The real creche, with its playrooms and learning devices was empty, he saw. No robots had been receiving post-awakening training. Sam was not surprised. Most of the work here had been devoted to research on the possibilities of robots. Actual construction was only a necessary sideline. Usually the brain complexes had been created and tested without bodies, and then extinguished before there had been a full awakening.

He started toward the educator computer out of his old habits. But it was only a machine that had programmed his progress from prepared tapes and memory circuits. It could not help him now.

Beyond the creche lay the heart of the whole affair. Here the brain complexes were assembled from components according to esoteric calculations. This was work that required a computer that was itself intelligent to some extent. It had to make sense out of the desirable options given it by men, then form the brain paths needed, either during construction or during the initial period before awakening. Everything that Sam had been before awakening had come from this. That pattern would still be recorded, along with what the great computer had learned of him during his return here five years before men abandoned the Moon.

Sam moved toward the machine, gazing in surprise at the amount of work lying about. There were boxes of robot bodies crammed into every storage space. They could never have been assembled in such numbers here during the period he remembered. And beyond lay shelves jammed with the components for the brain complexes. With such supplies, enough robots could be made to supply the Lunar Base needs for generations.

The computer itself was largely hidden far below, but its panel came to life at his touch. It waited.

"This is Robot Ninety-Three, Mark One," Sam said. "You have authorization on file."

The authorization from Dr. DeMatre should have been canceled. But the machine did not switch on alarm circuits. A thin cable of filaments reached out and passed into Sam's mouth slit. It retracted, and the speaker came to life. "There is authorization. What is wanted?"

"What is the correct date?" Sam asked. Then he grunted as the answer came from the machine's isotope clock.

It had been more than thirty-seven years since the men had left the Moon. He shook his head, and the robot bodies caught his attention again. "Why are so many robots being built?"

"Orders were received for one thousand robots trained to fly missiles. Orders were suspended by Director DeMatre. No orders have been received for removing parts."

"Do you know what happened to the men?" Sam had little hope of finding an easy answer any more, but he had to ask.

The machine seemed to hesitate. "Insufficient data. Orders were given by Director DeMatre to monitor broadcasts. Broadcasts were monitored. Analysis is incomplete. Data of doubtful coherence. Requests for more data were broadcast on all frequencies for six hours. Relevant replies were not received. Request further information if available."

"Never mind," Sam told it. "Can you teach me how to fly a plane?"

"Robot Ninety-Three, Mark One, was programmed with established ability to control all vehicles. Further instruction not necessary."

Sam grunted in amazement. He'd been surprised at how well he had controlled the landing craft and then the car. But it had never occurred to him that such knowledge had been built in.

"All right," he decided. "Start broadcasting again on all the frequencies you can handle. If you get any answers, find where the sender is and record it. If anyone asks who is calling, say you're calling for me and take any message. Tell them I'll be back in one month." He started to turn away, then remembered. "Finished for now."

The machine darkened. Sam headed out to find a field somewhere that might still have an operable plane. But he was already beginning to suspect what he would find.

VII

Grass grew and flowers bloomed. Ants built nests and crickets chirped in the soft summer night. The seas swarmed with marine life of most kinds. And reptiles sunned themselves on rocks, or retired to their holes when the sun was too hot.

But on all the Earth, no warm-blooded animal could be found.

The Earth of man was without form and void. The cities were slag heaps from which radioactivity still radiated. No fires burned on the hearthstones of the most isolated houses. The villages were usually burned, sometimes apparently by accident, but often as if they had been fired deliberately by their owners.

The Moon was a thing of glory over Lake Michigan. It was the only glorious thing for six hundred miles. Four returned winged rockets rested on a field in Florida, but there was no sign of what had become of the men who rode down from the station in them. One winged craft stood forlornly outside Denver, and there was a scrawl in crayon inside its port that spelled the worst obscenity in the English language.

There was a library still standing in Phoenix, and the last newspaper had the dateline of the day when Sam had seen the lights brighten over the cities of Earth. Most of the front page was occupied by a large box which advised its readers that the government had taken over all radio communications during the crisis and would broadcast significant news on the hour. The paper was cooperating with the government in making all such news available by broadcast only. The same box appeared in the nine preceding issues. Before that, the major news seemed to involve a political campaign in United South Africa.

Other scattered small libraries had papers that were no different. Yet the only clue was in one of those places. It was a piece of paper resting under the hand of a skeleton that was scattered before bound copies of a technical journal. The paper was covered with doodles and stained in what might have been blood. But the words were legible:

"Lesson for the day. Assign to all students. *Politics:* Men could not win such a war and that is obvious. *Chemistry:* Their nerve gas was similar to one we tested in small quantities. It seemed safe. Yet when they dropped it over us in both Northern and Southern hemispheres, it did not settle out as the test batches had done. *Proved,* that aerosols must be tested in massive quantities. *Medicine:* Bonny was in the shelter with me three weeks, yet there was still enough in the air to make her die in the ecstasy of a theophany. *Geography:* The wind patterns have been known for years. In three weeks, they reach all the Earth. *Psychology:* I am mad. But my madness is that I am become only cold logic without a soul. Therefore, I must kill myself. *Religion:* Nothing matters. I am mad. God is—"

That was all.

The creche was still the same, of course. Sam sat before the entrance three nights after his return to his only home on Earth, staring at the Moon that was rising over the horizon.

It was a full Moon again, and there was beauty to it, even here. But he was only vaguely aware of that. Below him, the great computer was quiescent now. It had taken all the mass of tiny details he had gathered and had integrated them with all of the millions of facts it already knew. Such a job had taken time, even for such a machine. But a few hours after his return it called him over the radio frequencies to issue its report.

"All data correlated," was its announcement. "Data not fully coherent with previous data. Degree of relevancy approaches zero. Data insufficient for conclusion."

Then it had gone back to stand-by, while Sam had sought the sight of living plants and insects outside the creche.

He had expected little else from the computer. He had known there was too little for a logical conclusion.

But his own conclusion was drawn now. As he sat under the light of the Moon, staring at the sky from which evil had come, there was a coldness in his brain complex that seemed deeper than the reaches of space.

Men were gone. He had faced that fact during the early days of his search, and now he was learning to live with it. There were no more of his creators. He would go on searching for them, of course, in the faint hope that a paltry few might have survived somehow, somewhere. But he was certain that the search would be in vain.

They had come from somewhere out there, he thought bitterly. The Eich, the minions of Boskone, or some other horror equally evil had appeared more than a century before and snooped and sniffed at Earth in their various saucers, only to leave. Now they had come back, giving Earth only a week's warning of their approach. They had struck all Earth with glowing bombs or radiation that ruined the cities of men. And when men still survived in spite of their rain of destruction, they had resorted to a deadly mist of insanity that was borne by the winds to every part of the planet. "They dropped it over us," the note had said. And the wonderful race Sam had known had died in madness, usually of some destructive kind.

There had not even been a purpose to it. *They* hadn't wanted the Earth for themselves. They had simply come and slaughtered, to depart as senselessly as they had departed before.

Sam beat his fist against his leg until the metal clanged through the night. Then he lifted his other fist toward the stars and shook it.

It was wrong that the alien invaders should escape from punishment.

They had come with fire and pestilence, and they should be found and overcome with all that they had meted out to mankind. He had supposed that evil was something found only in fiction. But now evil was ruler of the universe. It should be met as it was usually met in fiction. It should be wiped from existence in a suffering as great as it had inflicted. But such justice was apparently the one great lie of fiction.

He beat his fists resoundingly against his legs again and shouted at the Moon, but there was no relief for what was burning deep in him.

Then his ears picked up a new sound, and he stopped all motion to listen. It came again, very weakly and from very far away.

"Help!"

VIII

He shouted back audibly and by radio and was on his feet, running toward the sound. His feet crashed through the brush and he leaped over the rubble, making no effort to find the easy path. As he stopped to listen again, he heard the sound, directly ahead, but even weaker. A minute later he almost stumbled over the caller.

It was a robot. Once it had been slim and neat, covered with black enamel. Now it was bent and bare metal was exposed. But it was still a Mark Three. It lay without motion, only a whisper coming from its speaker.

Sam felt disappointment strike through all his brain complex, but he bent over the prone figure, testing quickly. It was power failure, he saw at once. He ripped a spare battery from the pack that had been with him during his long search and slammed it quickly into place, replacing the corroded one that had been there.

The little robot sat up and began trying to get to its feet. Sam reached out a helping hand, staring down at the worn, battered legs that seemed beyond any hope of functioning.

"You need help," he admitted. "You need a whole new body. Well, there are a thousand new ones going to waste in the creche, ready for you to use. What's your number?"

It had to be one of the robots from the Moon. Men had never permitted any robots to remain on Earth.

The robot teetered for a moment, then seemed to gain some mastery over its legs. "Joe. They called me Joe. I'm glad I heard your signal over the radio weeks ago, but it was a long way. My transmitter is broken. I couldn't answer you. A long way, and I was afraid I would fail before I could reach here. But now hurry. We can't waste time here."

"We'll hurry. But that way," Sam told him, pointing toward the creche.

Joe shook his head, making a creaking, horrible sound of it. "No, Sam. He can't wait. I think he's dying! He was sick when I heard the call from you, but he insisted I bring him here. He—"

"Sick? Dying? There's a *man* with you?"

Joe nodded jerkily and pointed.

Sam scooped the light figure up in his arms. Even on Earth, it was no great load for his larger body, and they could make much better time than by letting the other try to run. Hal, Sam thought. It was probably Hal. Hal had been the youngest. Hal would be only fifty-nine, or something like that. That wasn't too old for a man, from what he had learned.

He flicked his light on, unable to maintain full speed by the moonlight. The pointing finger of the other guided him down the slope to a worn, weed-covered trail. It was already more than five miles from the entrance to the creche.

"He was worried you might leave here before we could reach you," Joe explained. "He knew the month was almost up, and it might take too long for me to bring him. He ordered me to leave him and go ahead alone. Sometimes now it is hard to know whether he means what he says, but this was a clear order."

"You'd have been wiser to stick to the car and drive all the way with him," Sam suggested. He was forcing his way through a tangle of underbrush, wondering how much farther they had to go.

"There was no car," Joe said. "I can't drive one now. My arms sometimes stop working, and it would be dangerous to drive. I found a little wagon and dragged him behind me on that until we got here."

Sam took his eyes off the trail to stare at Joe's battered legs.

Joe had almost worn out his body. But in other ways, he must have developed a great deal since the days on the Moon. Time, experience and the companionship of men had shaped him far beyond what Sam remembered.

Then they were in a little hollow beside a brook, and there was a small tent pitched beside a cart. Sam released Joe and headed for the shelter. Moonlight broke through the trees and fell on the drawn suffering of a human face just inside the tent.

It took long study to find familiar features. At first nothing seemed right. Then Sam traced the jawline behind the long beard and gasped in recognition. "Dr. Smithers!"

"Hello, Sam." The eyes opened slowly, and a pain-racked smile stretched the lips briefly. "I was just dreaming about you. Thought you and Hal got lost in a crater. Better go shine up now. We'll want you to sing for us tonight. You're a good man, Sam, even if you are a robot. But you stay away too long out on those field trips."

Sam sighed softly. This was another reality he could recognize only from fiction. But he nodded. "Yes, Chief. It's all right now."

He began singing softly, the song about a Lady Greensleeves. A smile flickered over Smithers' lips again, and the eyes closed.

Then abruptly they snapped open, and Smithers tried to sit up. "Sam! You really are Sam! How'd you get here?"

Joe had been fussing over a little fire, drawing supplies from the cart. Now he hobbled up with a bowl of some broth and began trying to feed the man. Smithers swallowed a few mouthfuls dutifully, but his eyes remained on Sam. And he nodded as he heard the summary of the long struggle back to Earth. But when Sam told of the landing, he slumped back onto his pad.

"I'm glad you made it. Glad I got a chance to see you again before I give up the last ghost on Earth. I couldn't figure that radio signal Joe heard. Knew it couldn't be a human call, but I never thought of you making it back to Earth. Should have had a brass band to welcome you."

He closed his eyes, but the weak voice went on. "Hal and Randy died. Pete suicided. I'm the only one left, Sam. We waited up in the station three years, guessing what had happened here.

Then we came down and tried to find somebody—anybody—to start the race over. But there weren't any left. We covered every continent for thirty years. The robots got busted, except for Joe here. Then we came back. And now I'm the last man. The last man on Earth heard a knock on the door—and it was Sam. It's a better ending to the story than I expected."

He slept fitfully after that, though Sam could hear him moan at times. It was cancer, according to what Joe knew, and there was no hope.

Somehow, Joe had found a hospital with its equipment intact and books to study. The robot had taken Smithers there and tried to treat him with the equipment, but it had been a losing battle. Then, when the message came, broadcast by the computer at Sam's orders, Smithers had insisted on leaving. They had no radio capable of answering, and little hope of finding a working transmitter in time, so Smithers had insisted they must come in person. In the hospital, the treatment might have given him a year more of life; but he had ordered Joe to leave, knowing that he might not survive the trip. And now only his will seemed to keep the man alive. Joe had a few drugs to ease the pain, but that was all the help that could be given.

During the long night, Joe told more of the long search for survivors. It had been thorough. But they had found no trace of another living human being. The nerve gas had produced eventual death by nerve damage, as well as the initial insanity that had killed many.

"Who?" Sam asked bitterly. "What race did this?"

Joe made a gesture of uncertainty. "They talked about that. Mr. Norman told me about it, too. He explained that men killed each other off. One side attacked this side, and then our side had to hit back, until nobody was left. But I don't understand it."

"Do you believe it?"

"No," Joe answered. "Mr. Norman was always saying things I found he didn't really mean. No man would do anything like this."

Sam nodded, and began telling his theories. At first Joe was doubtful. Then the little robot seemed convinced. He dredged up small confirming bits of information from the long years of search. They weren't important by themselves, but a few seemed to add to the total picture. A sign cursed the "sky devils" in Borneo. There were odd bits from a sermon printed in Louisiana. And there were other vague hints at doom from beyond the Earth.

Twice during the long night Smithers wakened, but he was irrational. Sam soothed him and sang to him, while Joe tried to give him nourishment that was loaded with morphine. Now even Sam could see that the man was near death. The pulse was thready and the breathing seemed too much for the worn body.

In the morning, however, Smithers was rational again. He managed a smile. "Man goeth to his long home, and the mourners won't go about the streets this time. There won't be any mourners."

"There will be two," Sam told him.

"Yes." Smithers thought it over and nodded. "That's good, somehow. A man hates not being missed. I guess you two will have to take on all the debts of the human race now."

His breath caught sharply in his throat, and he retched weakly. But he forced himself up on his elbows and looked out through the flap of the tent toward the hills that showed through the shrubbery and the blue of the sky beyond.

"There are a lot of debts and a lot of broken promises, Sam, Joe," he said. "Man had promised to write some great things into the future of this universe. He was going to conquer the stars and even make a better scheme for everything. But he failed. He's finished. He dies, and the universe won't even know he's gone."

"We'll know," Joe said softly.

Smithers dropped back onto the pad. "Yeah. Maybe that helps. We had our faults, but I guess there must have been a lot of good in us, too—there had to be, if we could make two people like you. God, I'm tired!"

He closed his eyes. A few minutes later, Sam knew he was dead.

The two robots waited to be sure, and then wrapped the body in the tent and buried it, while Sam recited the scraps of the burial service he had picked up from his reading.

Sam sat down then where Smithers had died, staring at the world where no man would ever live again. And the knot in his brain complex grew stronger and colder. He could not see the stars in the light of the day. But he knew they were there. And somewhere out there was the debt Smithers had given him—a debt of justice that had to be paid.

Saucers, Boskone, the Eich—whatever they were, the evil alien monsters must be repaid to the last full measure for the foulness they had done and which man could no longer settle with them.

Anger and hate grew slowly in him against the enemy from the stars, until he could no longer contain his emotions. His radio message was almost a scream as he roused the computer.

"You've got a thousand robot bodies waiting. Can you build brains for them, modelled after the records of my brain? Can you build them without the limits you used for later models? Do you have materials for that?"

"Such a program is feasible," the machine answered.

"Then start—" Sam began. But his eyes fell on the wreck of Joe's body, and he modified his order. "No, save one body to replace another robot I'll bring you. Start work at once on all the others."

"The program is begun," the machine agreed.

Nine hundred and ninety-nine should be enough. They wouldn't be just like him, Sam realized; DeMatre had said there was a random factor. But they would do. The first group could find raw materials for ten thousand more, and those for still more. There would be robots enough to study all the books men had left, and to begin the long trip out into space.

This time, there would be more than a tape education for them. Sam would be there to tell them the story of man, the glory of the race, and the savage treachery that had robbed the universe of that race. They would learn that the universe held an enemy, a race of technological monsters that must be sought among the stars and exterminated to the last individual.

They would comb the entire galaxy for that enemy if they had to. And someday, mankind's debt of justice would be paid. Man would be avenged.

Sam looked up at the sky and foreswore all robots for all time to that debt of vengeance.

IX

Hate spewed across the universe in a high crusade. Metal ships leaped from star to star and hurtled across the immensities between the far-flung galaxies. The ships spawned incessantly, and with each went the holy image of their faith and the unsated and insatiable hunger of their hate.

A thousand stars yielded the dead and ancient wreckage of races that had once achieved technology. Five hundred suns gave light to intelligent races—quiet, peaceful races with backward cultures. The great ships dropped onto their worlds and went away again, leaving peoples throughout the galaxies filled with gratitude and paying homage to the incredibly beautiful images of the supernal being called Man. But still the quest went on.

In a great temple palace on the capital world of the Andromeda Galaxy, Sam stared down at a long table piled with little scraps of evidence. One graceful finger of his lithe seventeenth body stirred some of the scraps, and he bent closer to read what was left of the ancient writing. Then he looked up and across at the great scientist who had just returned from the ancient mother world of Earth, incredible light-years away.

"That is how the human race died?" Sam asked quietly. "You are quite sure?"

The scientist nodded. "Quite sure. Even with a hundred million workers, it took us fifty years to gather all this on Earth. It has been so badly scattered, so nearly ruined. But no truth from the past can be completely concealed from our present methods of research. Man died as I said."

Sam sighed softly and moved to the window. Outside it was summer, and the trees were in blossom, competing with the bright plumage of the birds brought from far Deneb. The gardens were a poem of color. He bent forward, sniffing the blended fragrance of the flowers. Strains of music came from the great Hall of Art that lifted its fairy beauty across the park. It was the eighth opus of their greatest living composer—an early work, but still magnificent in its reach and its ambition.

For the moment his shoulders slumped faintly. His emotions blended with the half-bitter memories of other discoveries. There had been the first visit to Mars—a Mars where no John Carter could ever have fought green men for the hand of the incredible Dejah Thoris. There had been star after star, with no friendly Arisians, no gallant dragon-folk to join against the undiscovered menace of Boskone. And for a thousand years, as fiction paled before reality, there had been the growing doubt in his mind. Now the last effort to make himself believe the legend he had created was spent.

"There is no Enemy now," the scientist said from behind him. "There can be no doubt. Man was his own destroyer. He killed himself. In a sense, his race was the one we are sworn to kill."

Sam leaned further out the window. Below, the throng of busy, laughing people looked up at him and cheered. There were a dozen races in the park, mingled with a majority of his people. He smiled and lifted his hand to them, then bent further out, until he could just see the great statue of Man that reared heavenward over the central part of the temple palace. He sighed again and inclined his head, before backing from the window.

"How many know this besides you, Robert?" he asked.

"None. It was gathered in too small fragments, until I could assemble it into a meaningful pattern."

Sam smiled at him. "Your work was well done, and there will be ways to reward you for it properly. But now I suggest that we burn this evidence."

"Burn it!" Robert's voice rose. "Burn this evidence and shackle our race to superstition forever? Our entire lives have been shaped to fit a cult of vengeance. Now we can free ourselves. This is our heritage, Sam—we can be ourselves!"

Sam ran his finger through the evidence again. There was pity in his mind for the scientist, but more for the strange race of man whose true nature had finally been revealed in fact. Man had missed owning the universe by so little! But the fates of that universe had conspired against him. The fates had offered two roads to intelligence. In one, there was the quiet growth that led to pastoral life and gentle pleasures, but somehow never got beyond its native planet. In the other, chosen by man, intelligence grew from the aggressions of savagery and thrust the race ahead to great discoveries—while building the means to the inevitable final aggression that must destroy itself utterly.

Man had failed, like all other races grown from killing strains of animal life. But in dying, he had passed on part of his soul to another race that had been designed without his mighty passions. Somehow he had passed on the driving anger of his spirit to his true children, the robots.

And they had carried on.

The robots had been a created race, a race designed only to serve, able to live in perfect peace and without ambition. They had owned no heritage. But through an accident of fiction and a few dying words, men had left them a rich heritage.

Anger had carried them throughout the stars, and hatred had bridged the spaces between the galaxies.

"You're mistaken, Robert," Sam said. "Vengeance *is* our heritage. Burn the evidence."

Most of the material was tinder dry, and it caught fire at the first spark. For a few seconds, it was a seething pillar of flame. Then there was only a dark scar on the wood to show the true death of man.

PROTOTAPH
Keith Laumer

One of the great concerns about computers is the question of privacy. With their incredible memories, computers can (if they are supplied with the proper information) instantly supply information about us to schools, police departments, and insurance companies. In fact, insurance companies make extensive use of computers in determining risk and insurance premium costs. In the following story, the author tells us about one young man's hair-raising encounter with a computer that can forecast the future.

I was already sweating bullets when I got to the Manhattan Life Concourse; then I had to get behind an old dame who spent a good half hour in the Policy Vending Booth, looking at little pieces of paper and punching the keys like they were fifty-credit bet levers at the National Lottery.

When I got in, I was almost scared to code my order into the Vendor; but I was scareder not to. I still thought maybe what happened over at Prudential and Gibraltar was some kind of fluke, even though I knew all the companies worked out of the Federal Actuarial Table Extrapolator; and Fate never makes a mistake.

But this had to be a mistake.

I punched the keys for a hundred thousand C's of Straight Life; nothing fancy, just a normal working-man's coverage. Then I shoved my ID in the slot and waited. I could feel sweat come out on my scalp and run down by my ear while I waited. I could hear the humming sound all around me like some kind of bees bottled up back of the big gray panel; then the strip popped out of the slot, and I knew what it said before I looked at it: UNINSURABLE.

I got the door open and shoved some guy out of my way and it was like I couldn't breathe. I mean, think about it: Twenty-one years old, out in the city to take my chances all alone, with no policy behind me. It was like the sidewalk under your feet turned to cracked ice, and no shore in sight.

A big expensive-looking bird in executive coveralls came out of a door across the lobby; I guess I yelled. Everybody was looking at me. When I grabbed his arm, he got that mad look and started to reach for his lapel button—the kind that goes with a Million Cee Top Crust policy.

"You got to listen," I told him. "I tried to buy my insurance—and all I got was this!" I shoved the paper in his face. "Look at me," I told him. "I'm healthy, I'm single, I finished Class Five Subtek school yesterday, I'm employed! What do you mean, uninsurable?"

"Take your hands off me," he said in a kind of choky voice. He was looking at the paper, though. He took it and gave me a look like he was memorizing my face for picking out of a line-up later.

"Your ID," he held out his hand and I gave it to him. He looked at it and frowned an important-looking frown.

"Hm-m-m. Seems in order. Possibly some, er..." He pushed his mouth in and out and changed his mind about saying it; he knew as well as I did that the big actuarial computer doesn't make mistakes. "Come along," he turned his back and headed for the lift bank.

"What have I got, some kind of incurable disease or something?" I was asking them; they just looked at me and goggled their eyes. More of them kept coming in, whispering together; then they'd hurry away and here would come a new bunch. And none of them told me anything.

"The old crock in front of me, she was ninety if she was a day!" I told them. "She got her policy! Why not me?"

They didn't pay any attention. Nobody cared about me; how I felt. I got up and went over to the first guy that had brought me up here.

"Look," I said. I was trying to sound reasonable. "What I mean is, even a guy dying in the hospital can get a policy for *some* premium. It's the law; everybody's got a right to be insured. And—"

"I know the laws governing the issuance of policies by this company," the man barked at me. He was sweating, too. He got out a big tissue and patted himself with it. He looked at a short fat man with a stack of papers in his hand.

"I don't care what kind of analysis you ran," he told him. "Run another one. Go all the way back to Primary if you have to, but get to the bottom of this! I want to know why this"—he gave me a look—"this individual is unique in the annals of actuarial history!"

"But, Mr. Tablish—I even coded in a trial run based on a

one hundred per cent premium, with the same result: No settlement of such a claim is possible—"

"I'm not interested in details; just get me results! The computer has available to it every fact in the known universe; see that it divulges the reasoning behind this...this anomaly!"

The fat man went away. They took me to another room and a doctor ran me through the biggest med machine I ever saw. When he finished I heard him tell the big man I was as sound as a Manhattan Term Policy.

That made me feel a little better—but not much.

Then the fat man came back, and his face was a funny white color—like some raw bread I saw once on a field trip through Westside Rationing. He said something to the others, and they all started to talk at once, and some of them were yelling now. But do you think any of them told me anything? I had to wait another hour, and then a tall man with white hair came in and everybody got quiet and he looked at papers and they all got their heads together and muttered; and then they looked at me, and I felt my heart pounding up under my ribs and I was feeling sick then, med machine or no med machine.

Then they told me.

That was two days ago. They got me in this room now, a fancy room up high in some building. There're guys around to do whatever I want—servants, I guess you'd call 'em. They gave me new clothes, and the food—West Rat never put out anything like this. No liquor, though—and no smokes. And when I said I wanted to go out, all I got was a lot of talk. They treat me—careful. Not like they like me, you know, but like I was a bomb about to go off. It's a funny feeling. I guess I got more power than anybody that ever lived—more power than you can even get your mind around the thought of. But a lot of good it does me. There's only the one way I can use it—and when I think about that, I get that sick feeling again.

And meanwhile, I can't even go for a walk in the park.

The president was here just now. He came in, looking just like the Tri-D, only older, and he came over and looked at me kind of like I looked at him. I guess it figures: There's only one of each of us.

"Are you certain there's not some...some error, George?" he said to the wrinkly-faced man that walked just behind him.

"The Actuarial Computer is the highest achievement of a thousand years of science, Mr. President," he said in a deep voice like the mud on the bottom of the ocean. "Our society is based on the concept of its infallibility within the physical laws of the Universe. Its circuits are capable of analyses and perceptions that range into realms of knowledge as far beyond human awareness as is ours beyond that of a protozoan. An error? No, Mr. President."

He nodded. "I see." That's all he said. Then he left.

Now I'm sitting here. I don't know what to do next—what to say. There's a lot to this—and in a way, there's nothing. I got to think about it, dope it out. There's got to be something I can do— but what?

The machine didn't say much. They took me down to the subvault where the big voice panel is located and where the primary data goes in, and let me hear for myself. It didn't give any explanations; it just told me.

Funny; in a way it was like something I've always known, but when you hear Fate come right out and say it, it's different.

When I die, the world ends.

DIAL "F" FOR FRANKENSTEIN

Arthur C. Clarke

The telephone is one of humankind's greatest inventions. It allows us to chat with friends and relatives thousands of miles away, brings us help in an emergency, and can be used to conduct important business transactions. But in this story by Arthur C. Clarke, the telephone calls *us*, with some very bad news indeed.

At 0150 Greenwich Mean Time on December 1, 1975, every telephone in the world started to ring. A quarter of a billion people picked up their receivers to listen for a few seconds with annoyance or perplexity. Those who had been awakened in the middle of the night assumed that some far-off friend was calling over the satellite telephone network that had gone into service, with such a blaze of publicity, the day before. But there was no voice on the line, only a sound that to many seemed like the roaring of the sea—to others, like the vibrations of harp strings in the wind. And there were many more, in that moment, who recalled a sound of childhood—the noise of blood pulsing through the veins, heard when a shell is cupped over the ear. Whatever it was, it lasted no more than 20 seconds; then it was replaced by the dialing tone.

The world's subscribers cursed, muttered, "Wrong number," and hung up. Some tried to dial a complaint, but the line seemed busy. In a few hours, everyone had forgotten the incident—except those whose duty it was to worry about such things.

At the Post Office Research Station, the argument had been going on all morning and had got nowhere. It continued unabated through the lunch break, when the hungry engineers poured into the little café across the road.

"I still think," said Willy Smith, the solid-state electronics man, "that it was a temporary surge of current, caused when the satellite network was switched in."

"It was obviously *something* to do with the satellites," agreed Jules Reyner, circuit designer. "But why the time delay? They were plugged in at midnight; the ringing was two hours later—as we all know to our cost." He yawned violently.

"What do *you* think, Doc?" asked Bob Andrews, computer programmer. "You've been very quiet all morning. Surely you've got some idea?"

Dr. John Williams, head of the mathematics division, stirred uneasily.

"Yes," he said, "I have. But you won't take it seriously."

"That doesn't matter. Even if it's as crazy as those science-fiction yarns you write under a pseudonym, it may give us some leads."

Williams blushed, but not very hard. Everyone knew about his stories, and he wasn't ashamed of them. After all, they *had* been collected in book form. (Remainder at five shillings; he still had a couple of hundred copies.)

"Very well," he said, doodling on the tablecloth. "This is something I've been wondering about for years. Have you ever considered the analogy between an automatic telephone exchange and the human brain?"

"Who hasn't thought of it?" scoffed one of his listeners. "That idea must go back to Graham Bell."

"Possibly; I never said it was original. But I do say it's time we started taking it seriously." He squinted balefully at the fluorescent tubes above the table; they were needed on this foggy winter day. "What's wrong with the damn lights? They've been flickering for the last five minutes."

"Don't bother about that; Maisie's probably forgotten to pay her electricity bill. Let's hear more about your theory."

"Most of it isn't theory; it's plain fact. We know that the human brain is a system of switches—neurons—interconnected in a very elaborate fashion by nerves. An automatic telephone exchange is also a system of switches—selectors, and so forth—connected together with wires."

"Agreed," said Smith. "But that analogy won't get you very far. Aren't there about fifteen billion neurons in the brain? That's a lot more than the number of switches in an autoexchange."

Williams's answer was interrupted by the scream of a low-flying jet; he had to wait until the café had ceased to vibrate before he could continue.

"Never heard them fly *that* low," Andrews grumbled. "Thought it was against regulations."

"So it is, but don't worry—London Airport Control will catch him."

"I doubt it," said Reyner. "That *was* London Airport, bringing in a Concorde on ground approach. But I've never heard one so low, either. Glad I wasn't aboard."

"Are we, or are we *not,* going to get on with this blasted discussion?" demanded Smith.

"You're right about the fifteen billion neurons in the human brain," continued Williams, unabashed. "And *that's* the whole point. Fifteen billion sounds like a large number, but it isn't. Round about the 1960s, there were more than that number of individual switches in the world's autoexchanges. Today, there are approximately five times as many."

"I see," said Reyner very slowly. "And as of yesterday, they've all become capable of full interconnection, now that the satellite links have gone into service."

"Precisely."

There was silence for a moment, apart from the distant clanging of a fire-engine bell.

"Let me get this straight," said Smith. "Are you suggesting that the world telephone system is now a giant brain?"

"That's putting it crudely—anthropomorphically. I prefer to think of it in terms of critical size." Williams held his hands out in front of him, fingers partly closed.

"Here are two lumps of U 235; nothing happens as long as you keep them apart. But bring them together"—he suited the action to the words—"and you have something *very* different from one bigger lump of uranium. You have a hole half a mile across.

"It's the same with our telephone networks; until today they've been largely independent, autonomous. But now we've suddenly multiplied the connecting links—the networks have all merged together—and we've reached criticality."

"And just what does criticality mean in this case?" asked Smith.

"For want of a better word—consciousness."

"A weird sort of consciousness," said Reyner. "What would it use for sense organs?"

"Well, all the radio and TV stations in the world would be feeding information into it, through their landlines. *That* should give it something to think about! Then there would be all the data stored in all the computers; it would have access to that—and to the electronic libraries, the radar tracking systems, the telemetering in the automatic factories. Oh, it would have enough sense organs! We can't begin to imagine its picture of the world, but it would certainly be infinitely richer and more complex than ours."

"Granted all this, because it's an entertaining idea," said Reyner, "what could it *do* except think? It couldn't go anywhere; it would have no limbs."

"Why should it want to travel? It would already be everywhere! And every piece of remotely controlled electrical equipment on the planet could act as a limb."

"Now I understand that time delay," interjected Andrews. "It was conceived at midnight, but it wasn't born until one-fifty this morning. The noise that woke us all up was—its birth cry."

His attempt to sound facetious was not altogether convincing, and nobody smiled. Overhead, the lights continued their annoying flicker, which seemed to be getting worse. Then there was an interruption from the front of the café as Jim Small of Power Supplies made his usual boisterous entry.

"Look at this, fellows," he grinned, waving a piece of paper in front of his colleagues. "I'm rich. Ever seen a bank balance like *that?*"

Dr. Williams took the proffered statement, glanced down the columns and read the balance aloud: "Credit £999,999,897.87.

"Nothing very odd about that," he continued above the general amusement. "I'd say it means the computer's made a slight mistake. That sort of thing was happening all the time just after the banks converted to the decimal system."

"I know, I know," said Jim, "but don't spoil my fun. I'm going to frame this statement—and what would happen if I drew a check for a few million on the strength of this? Could I sue the bank if it bounced?"

"Not on your life," answered Reyner. "I'll take a bet that the banks thought of *that* years ago and protected themselves somewhere down in the small print. But by the way—when did you get that statement?"

"In the noon delivery; it comes straight to the office, so that my wife doesn't have a chance of seeing it."

"Hmm—that means it was computed early this morning. Certainly after midnight...."

"What are you driving at? And why all the long faces?"

No one answered him; he had started a new hare, and the hounds were in full cry.

"Does anyone here know about automated banking systems?" asked Willy Smith. "How are they tied together?"

"Like everything else these days," said Bob Andrews. "They're all in the same network—the computers talk to one another all over the world. It's a point for you, John. If there *was* real trouble, that's one of the first places I'd expect it. Besides the phone system itself, of course."

"No one answered the question I asked before Jim came in," complained Reyner. "What would this supermind actually *do*? Would it be friendly—hostile—indifferent? Would it even know that we exist, or would it consider the electronic signals it's handling to be the only reality?"

"I see you're beginning to believe me," said Williams with a certain grim satisfaction. "I can only answer your question by asking another. What does a newborn baby do? It starts looking for food." He glanced up at the flickering lights. "My God," he said slowly, as if a thought had just struck him. "There's only one food it would need—electricity."

"This nonsense has gone far enough," said Smith. "What the devil's happened to our lunch? We ordered twenty minutes ago."

Everyone ignored him.

"And then," said Reyner, taking up where Williams had left off, "it would start looking around and stretching its limbs. In fact, it would start to play, like any growing baby."

"And babies *break* things," said someone softly.

"It would have enough toys, heaven knows. That Concorde that went over just now. The automated production lines. The traffic lights in our streets."

"Funny you should mention that," interjected Small. "Something's happened to the traffic outside—it's been stopped for the last ten minutes. Looks like a big jam."

"I guess there's a fire somewhere—I heard an engine."

"I've heard two—and what sounded like an explosion over toward the industrial estate. Hope it's nothing serious."

"Maisie!!! What about some candles? We can't see a thing!"

"I've just remembered—this place has an all-electric kitchen. We're going to get cold lunch, if we get any lunch at all."

"At least we can read the newspaper while we're waiting. Is that the latest edition you've got there, Jim?"

"Yes—haven't had time to look at it yet. Hmm—there *do* seem to have been a lot of odd accidents this morning—railway signals jammed—water main blown up through failure of relief valve—dozens of complaints about last night's wrong numbers——"

He turned the page and became suddenly silent.

"What's the matter?"

Without a word, Small handed over the paper. Only the front page made sense. Throughout the interior, column after column was a mass of printer's pie—with, here and there, a few incongruous advertisements making islands of sanity in a sea of gibberish. They had obviously been set up as independent blocks and had escaped the scrambling that had overtaken the text around them.

"So this is where long-distance typesetting and autodistribution have brought us," grumbled Andrews. "I'm afraid Fleet Street's been putting too many eggs in one electronic basket."

"So have we all, I'm afraid," said Williams very solemnly. "So have we all."

"If I can get a word in edgeways, in time to stop the mob hysteria which seems to be infecting this table," said Smith loudly and firmly, "I'd like to point out that there's nothing to worry about— even if John's ingenious fantasy is correct. We only have to switch off the satellites—and we'll be back where we were yesterday."

"Prefrontal lobotomy," muttered Williams. "I'd thought of that."

"Eh? Oh, yes—cutting out slabs of the brain. That would certainly do the trick. Expensive, of course, and we'd have to go back to sending telegrams to each other. But civilization would survive."

From not too far away, there was a short, sharp explosion.

"I don't like this," said Andrews nervously. "Let's hear what the old BBC's got to say—the one-o'clock news has just started."

He reached into his briefcase and pulled out a transistor radio.

"—unprecedented number of industrial accidents, as well as the unexplained launching of three salvos of guided missiles from military installations in the United States. Several airports have had to suspend operations owing to the erratic behavior of their radars, and the banks and stock exchanges have closed because their information-processing systems have become completely unreliable." ("You're telling me," muttered Small, while the others shushed him.) "One moment, please—there's a news flash coming through.... Here it is. We have just been informed that all control over the newly installed communication satellites has been lost. They are no longer responding to commands from the ground. According to——"

The BBC went off the air; even the carrier wave died. Andrews reached for the tuning knob and twisted it round the dial. Over the whole band, the ether was silent.

Presently Reyner said, in a voice not far from hysteria, "That prefrontal lobotomy was a good idea, John. Too bad that baby's already thought of it."

Williams rose slowly to his feet.

"Let's get back to the lab," he said. "There must be an answer somewhere."

But he knew already that it was far, far too late. For Homo sapiens, the telephone bell had tolled.

THE OTHER SIDE

Walter Kubilius

Walter Kubilius has written only a small number of science fiction stories over the years, but almost all of them have been memorable, perhaps none more so than this beautiful little gem about a boy, machines, and the true meaning of loneliness.

Jim Carrington splashed in the waters of Hillsboro's only river, only a few feet away from the Wall, and taunted his play-mates. None of them could swim, and once when he tried to push Jack Baker into the river his only response was violent fear.

"Fraidy cats!" Jim yelled. He saw a speckled trout swim by and then dove down for it. He bruised himself on the rocks in the river and as he scrambled upward the palm of his hand struck the bottom of the Wall. *The palm of his hand struck the bottom of the Wall!* It was no more than an inch thick and if he had wanted to he could have swum right under it, and into the forbidden Outside.

"You know we're not supposed to be near the Wall," Baker said, "the radiation is liable to kill us."

"Nuts," Jim said, scrambling up the grassy bank, "If there was any radiation...oh, forget it." He was about to say that if there was any actual atomic radiation outside the water would be poi-sonous and the fish would be contaminated and deadly. Yet he had been drinking that water and eating the fish as long as he could remember. There was no poison, even though they came from the forbidden Outside. Ergo, the schoolbooks were all wrong.

He dressed quickly, picked up his textbooks and raced the boys back to Hillsboro. Pop was at the tractor wheel as usual, his farmer's eye upon that sun which looked like a burning piece of paper plastered against the Wall. The sun was 93,000,000 miles away, so the books said, but to Jim it still looked as if it were a part of the Wall.

"Have a good time?" Pop asked. He always asked the same question in the same way, just as Mom always had their meals ready in the same way. "Oh, it was all right," Jim said, "but I sure wish that Baker would break his neck. He gives me a pain."

He put his books in the barn and then did some of the farm chores, feeding the pigs, chickens, cows, and horses. "Pop," he asked when his father came back from the field, "why do you keep the horses since you never use them? You might as well sell them."

Pop thought for a moment. "Don't rightly know," he said, "We farmers always have horses. Do they bother you?"

"No, Pop."

Old Doc Barnes, Hillsboro's one and only practitioner, visited the farm on the following night and put Jim through another one of his rigorous examinations. He listened to Jim's heart, took samples of his blood and sweat and examined them under a portable microscope and then made notations in a large black book that had Jim's name on the front cover.

"Perfect health," Doc Barnes said as he unstrapped the pressure belt and started packing his instruments back into the three bags he brought with him. "As sound as Robinson's election program, and nothing wrong with you that fried steak and mashed potatoes can't cure."

Jim dressed. "Why do you examine me so often?" he asked.

Doc Barnes looked surprised. "Why, son, we've got socialized medicine now that Robinson's elected. It's the law, you know. Didn't you learn it in school?"

"Yes, I know," Jim said, "but why is it you never examine Pop? He's a citizen, too. Yet you only worry about me."

There was a flicker of doubt in the doctor's eyes and then the same, kind, cheerful voice. "Why, of course I do! You're simply not around when I examine your father and mother. In fact, I'm glad you reminded me so I can give them a good physical checkup. We need it every month, you know."

"Sure," Jim said. When the Doc went to Pop's bedroom an idea flashed through the boy's mind. In a sense it was spying, but the suspicion that something was wrong in Doc Barnes' hearty friendliness had long bothered Jim. It was nothing that he could identify. Was there something wrong with Jim that made the doctor so concerned with him? He spent two or three hours on Jim's monthly examination. At most he could examine five people a day, or a hundred and fifty a month. A hundred and fifty a month! There were about 10,000 people in Hillsboro and Doc Barnes was the only doctor he had ever heard of.

He went quietly upstairs to the attic and pushed back a bookcase covering a wide crack in the floor. By bending down he could see through to the floor beneath and hear the conversation.

"The boy has asked why I do not examine you," Doc Barnes was saying, his voice flat and monotonous. "We will stay here for a while to satisfy him."

Then they remained sitting like stone statues in immovable chairs—Mom, Pop, and Doc Barnes.

Jim crept silently down the stairs to the porch and waited patiently until Doc Barnes left the house.

"Did you examine the folks?" Jim asked.

"I sure did," Doc Barnes said, "Gave 'em the most thorough examination I ever gave anybody. You can rest assured, son, there's not a thing wrong with them." He patted Jim on the shoulders and then went back to his car and rode into town. Jim watched him go before going into the parlor. Doc Barnes did not stop at a single other farmhouse on the road.

"Here's today's paper, son," Pop said, giving him the copy of the *Hillsboro Daily Chronicle*. There was no world news on this January 15, 1993, and President Robinson and Vice-President Koshbino spent the day giving tedious reports on the economic recovery program. It was the local news which hit Jim like a brick thrown into his face. Jack Baker was dead. He had fallen from a tree and broken his neck. Jim felt sick.

"Sold the horses today," Pop said, "Made a good profit on them."

"That's swell," Jim said, the words like sawdust in his mouth. His head was whirling. His eyes could no longer focus on the words of the newspaper, and the vague suspicion he had long been feeling approached one more step towards final understanding. He knew that Jack Baker never swam and, what was much more important, never climbed trees, and the knowledge that he had wished for his death made him feel like a murderer. Like some rumbling out of a whirling void, he heard his father's voice, "How are you getting on at school?"

"I hate it," Jim said, the tension in him breaking out and the accumulation of many doubts making themselves heard. "It's the other boys. I—I can't explain it. They either know too much, or not enough. I think I could learn more by myself in the library."

As soon as the anger broke, it flurried and died and soon the incident was forgotten. He did the chores around the farm and spent his free time swimming in the river at a spot where the banks widened near the Wall. He did not dive near the Wall, nor attempt to pass under it to the Outside, where poisoned fumes and deadly gases scorched the ground and made one breath of air a sentence of death. Yet the water was clear and good.

A few days later Pop gave him a letter from the Board of Education for Hillsboro. It was a brief announcement declaring that because of increased tax contributions to the nation's recovery program, Hillsboro had to reduce its appropriations for education. The school was hereby closed, and those students who wished could secure adult privileges at the Public Library, where Miss Wilson would be glad to confer with them.

It was the sort of privilege that Jim had long dreamed of. His hungry eyes had often feasted upon the long galleries of bookshelves, all lined with thick layers of dust as if the knowledge of all the Earth had been stored here and forgotten. In their pages he would find the answers to Baker's death, the dishonesty of Doc Barnes, and perhaps even the mystery of the Wall and what was really outside.

Miss Wilson, head librarian for the adult division, was a thin, white-faced woman with the same kind of blank smile that Doc Barnes wore. She perched on a high stool beside her desk at the entrance. "What would you like to read?" she asked, "I have here a very good book on natural history which you might like, or would you prefer some adult fiction? Here is a splendid—"

"If it's all right, I'd like to just look around for myself."

"—novel about farm life and how a young man developed a process that doubled his agricultural yield."

"May I go in?" Jim asked, exasperated by the long lecture

which droned from Miss Wilson's lips. She stopped suddenly, looked blankly at him as if listening to someone, and then smiled.

"Of course. You can take out any books that you like. Do you know how to use the catalogue?"

"Yes, yes." Jim said, hurriedly moving into the deserted library. The long rows of book stacks stretched almost endlessly through the huge vaulted chamber. Jim's nose twitched at the pleasant musty odor of age that clung about the cloth and leather-bound volumes. He studied some of the titles, pulled the books from the shelves and with a gusty breath blew off the layer of dust upon the fore-edge and flicked through the pages. The books of fiction, which occupied more than half the shelves, did not interest him. He wandered through the sections on science and particularly through the 900's, where the history books were. Unlike the fiction books that were practically untouched, there were huge empty spaces in the shelves, bright exposed metal gleaming where numbers of books had been suddenly removed.

On some of the books there were curious scratches upon the dusty covers, as if oddly shaped hands had picked them up and then decided to put them back upon the shelves.

"Perhaps," Jim said, "the books about the Wall are classified separately."

He went to the rows of catalogue drawers in the center of the library and pulled out the one labelled Wa-Wun. There were no books on the subject of the Wall or any title carrying information about it. There were several that carried the word "Outside" in them, but none of the books dealt with what Hillsboro meant when "Outside" was mentioned. He thought there might be some other term for "Wall" that he had not heard, and he began to look through the listings of "Screen," "Ceiling," "Barrier," "Barricade," and everything he could think of or find in the dictionaries. The catalogue seemed to be thorough, even though quite a number of the index cards had been ripped out, as he could tell by the scraps of paper remaining, but there was nothing about the Wall in any of them.

Dismayed, he tried to be satisfied with a few history books and brought them to Miss Wilson for recording.

She glanced at the titles, smiled brightly, and stamped the due dates on his card. "Find everything you want?" she asked.

"No," he said, somewhat angry as he slipped the books under his arm, "I couldn't find anything about the Wall."

Her smile faded. "The Wall?"

"Yes," he exclaimed, irritated at what was clearly some sort of effort to hide the truth from him, "The Wall, Ceiling, Dome, whatever you want to call it, that's all around Hillsboro. Why doesn't anyone ever mention it? I wouldn't have even known it was there if I didn't go swimming near it. There's not a single book about it in the whole library."

Miss Wilson regained her composure. "Of course there is," she said very sweetly as if talking to an unreasonable child. "Have you tried the catalogue?"

"Yes, and there's no card for it."

"You must be mistaken," she said. "I'll help you look for it when you return next week."

"Sure," Jim said, certain that some sort of excuse would be found. He sensed the existence of a strange conspiracy. What was there to hide?

"Pop," he asked after the evening chores were done and they were seated on the porch, listening to the crickets and watching the clouds roll by the face of the moon, "just what is the Wall?"

Pop put down his paper and looked speculatively off toward the horizon where the translucent Wall dug into the earth just beyond that line of hills. "It was there long before you was born," he said, "Sort of a defense against the Outside, if I remember rightly."

"What's Outside?" Jim asked quietly.

Pop picked up his paper and started reading to show that he didn't feel like talking much. "Heck, everybody knows that. Poison gas and gamma radiations and stuff like that. It'd kill everybody if it got in."

Jim thought of the clean fresh water and the healthy fish that flowed from under the Wall. He wanted to ask Pop, but the newspaper was now a barrier between them.

There was not enough light to read by, so Jim looked out across the fields and up to the inverted Dome through which the stars could be seen. There seemed to be peace and contentment outside and not the death and horror his father hinted at. When Pop left the porch, Jim took his place under the lamp and read through the history books. Most of them were very old, dating back to 1970. Since there was no mention of the Wall in them or the atomic wars which made the Wall necessary, Jim concluded that the Wall was built between 1970 and '75, when he was born.

Jim picked up the next book, "History of the United Nations," published in 1992. It was only one year old yet had the strange appearance of great age, the pages stained and crinkly. He looked closely at the title page and read the small print that made his heart pound. "Ninth edition," the tiny letters said, "Revised and corrected by the author, January 2039."

It's a misprint, Jim reasoned, *for this is only 1993.* Nevertheless he turned hastily towards the back pages and began reading:

> F. M. Robinson, during whose presidential administration the United Nations secured a lasting peace, died in a rocket crash in 2001. Koshbino served as president until the expiration of his term in 2002, and the election of Ghafa Benjamin occurred the following year.
>
> During Ghafa's administration the Planet Commission continued its efforts to build a successful extra-galactic vessel but these were without success until 2038.
>
> The gradual elimination of farming communities, begun during Robinson's term as president, continued under the new administration. The artificial manufacture of food by reprocessing industrial waste had revolutionized social customs, particularly in the frequent distressing economic dislocations—

Jim Carrington put the book aside, bewildered by the massive history of great events which were yet to occur. President Robinson was alive, for he had seen his calm, dignified face on the television screen many times. As for the artificial manufacture of food supposedly convulsing the nation's economy, there was not the slightest evidence of it in Hillsboro. Pop plowed the field with his tractor and the wheat, oats, and rye were delivered to town where they were stored in warehouses, presumably for shipment to other Wall-surrounded cities. If food could be manufactured, there was no point in growing it here. If it could not be manufactured, then the history book was some sort of fraud.

He hurriedly skimmed through the pages, searching for some reasonable explanation. The more he read, the more confused he became. There was no mention of any worldwide atomic conflagration in 1970 and not the slightest indication anywhere that Wall-enclosed cities existed or were ever considered.

There were creaking sounds in the driveway, and Jim looked up to see Doc Barnes' battered car come to a stop. The medic waved to him, and then came puffing up the porch steps. "Evenin', Jim," he said. "Thought I'd drop by and say hello."

"Pop and Mom are in the parlor if you want to see them."

Doc Barnes eased himself with a grunt into the porch rocking chair and wiped his sweating forehead with a rumpled handkerchief. "Nothing important," he said, "just returning from a call and thought I'd drop by and rest a while." He glanced around him and saw the books on the floor beside Jim. "Been reading a lot, son?"

"Yes," Jim said cautiously, "a couple of history books."

"Never could see anything interesting in history," Doc Barnes said. "I always felt the physical sciences had more challenge in them. There's nothing more thrilling than examining a bug under a microscope. Come down to my lab sometime and I'll show you some fascinating aspects of scientific research."

Doc Barnes talked on, and the guarded suspicion which Jim felt gradually faded away. He scarcely understood half the words the doctor used in explaining the anatomy of atoms and how molecular velocities could be measured.

"History has no meaning," Doc Barnes said, "and you'll never find truth there. Study the sciences, where all evidence can be weighed and measured. It's the only road to truth."

"What is the Wall?" Jim asked suddenly.

"Crushed matter," Doc Barnes said unhesitatingly. "It's a mixture of bare nuclei and free, unattached electrons. Ordinarily such an electronic gas would expand and dissipate but for layers of transparent matter which keep it within set confines. The wall is then completely impenetrable to everything but harmless sun and starlight, and yet it can be touched without danger. It was built in 1975, during the planet-wide war which rendered so much land radioactively dangerous."

"If that's true," Jim said, knowing that the moment of decision had come, "why is it there's no mention of the Wall or even the war in this history book?"

He opened the book triumphantly and passed it over to the doctor. He did not know the elements of the conspiracy, but he was sure that Doc Barnes was part of it. The Wall was an important element of their lives yet there was never any mention of it in the library which was supposed to hold the sum of human knowledge. Doc Barnes' face was set and hard as he read the pages that Jim opened before him. He flipped the leaves, glancing at the years marked at the head of each page—1970—1980—1990—1995—2000—2035. It was not only a history of the past, it was a history of the future as well, and nowhere was there any mention of the Wall.

"What year is this?" Jim demanded. Here at last was his chance to grope with the mystery of his life. Who was he? What was he? As a boy he remembered nothing but Pop and Mom in the Hillsboro farm, but as he grew older he began to realize certain inconsistencies. His slightest wishes seemed to become automatic law. He recalled how Doc Barnes seemed to live only to look after Jim, and how the whole town of Hillsboro was joined in a conspiracy to keep him in ignorance of certain things. Perhaps he was imagining these things—but they had become too frequent. This book was the first proof he had found for his suspicions. It clearly proved that not only was there no Atomic War and no need for a Wall, but that even the date was a lie.

"What year is this?" he demanded again.

"1993, of course," Doc Barnes said, uneasily.

"Then what is this book?" Jim asked, almost violently. "Is it possible to foretell the future?"

"Of course not," Doc Barnes said, "the future is closed to us.

As for this book, I'm sorry that it disturbed you for it is obviously a hoax. It was probably published as some sort of college thesis in speculative history. That is frequently done in some of the universities, the idea being to test the applicant and see whether he has mastered the various theories of social history. Economic and anthropologic factors as determinants in history are considered quite valid in some colleges. Incidentally, Jim, would you like to go to college a year or so from now? I have some friends at Harvard and they might accept you."

Jim tore the book from Doc Barnes' hands. "You're not telling me the truth!" he said hotly. "This is no Ph.D. thesis or even any attempt at hoaxing somebody. It's a textbook, pure and simple, only it's a textbook from the future that does not mention any Atomic War or any Wall around Hillsboro or any other place. Why isn't the Wall mentioned anywhere else? I've looked through all the history books in the library and nowhere is the Wall even hinted at. Why?"

"Oh, come now," Doc Barnes said, reaching into his medical kit and fumbling for some instrument. "I'm sure you're mistaken. When you visit the library again, ask one of the attendants to help you."

Jim watched Doc Barnes' hand come out of the black bag. Between fore and index fingers was the transparent body of a hypodermic, with a thumb securely placed against the plunger.

"What are you going to do?" Jim asked, becoming afraid. "Nothing important," Doc Barnes said. "These are some vitamins. They will help improve your appetite."

"My appetite is all right," Jim said, slowly standing up and stepping back to the porch wall. Doc Barnes also arose and stepped near him.

"Don't be afraid," Doc Barnes said. "This won't hurt at all."

Jim ducked beneath the upraised arm, kicking aside the books that littered the porch. He was not fast enough, and Doc's arm plunged down and the needle jabbed into his shoulder. "Pop! Mom!" he screamed, and then tumbled into darkness.

In the morning Jim arose and had breakfast with Pop, wondering if the events of last night were only a dream. "Doc Barnes was here last night," he said to his father.

"Yeah?" Pop said, "I didn't hear him."

"We had a long talk," Jim said doubtfully. "I—I think I fainted."

"Maybe you been reading too much," Pop said, "You looked all right when I saw you go to bed."

Jim finished the rest of his meal in silence. On the porch he picked up four library books, the fifth being missing, and returned them to the library.

Instead of Miss Wilson there was a young, round-faced man in a steel gray suit at the recording desk. He took Jim's books and stamped his library card.

"She's no longer here," he said in answer to Jim's question. "The Board transferred her to another library. Inefficient, I understand, for many of the books were misplaced on the shelves and entered incorrectly in the catalogue."

Jim took his card and looked on the "due" list. "I still have one book home," he said.

The librarian shook his head. "You must be mistaken. You've returned all the books listed on your card. What is the title?"

"History of the United Nations."

The librarian studied a list before him. "I'm sorry, but there's no such book listed. Do you know when it was published?"

Jim bit his lip. "2038."

The librarian smiled. "You are joking, of course."

Knowing further talk would be useless, Jim went into the library. That book would never be found, he knew, for Doc Barnes had taken it. The "vitamin" injection was only a sedative to enable the doctor to steal the book and make Jim think the whole incident a dream. The new librarian was also part of the conspiracy around him, just as Miss Wilson had been. He had learned one thing in his talk with Doc Barnes, and that was not to trust anyone. For all he knew every man and woman in Hillsboro, not excepting his own father and mother, was part of that mysterious alliance to keep him from learning the truth—whatever that truth might be.

He went to the catalogue drawers, determined to make one final search for some book that might have a passing reference to the Wall or the Atomic War that necessitated its construction. The chance remark of the new librarian that Miss Wilson was inefficient had prepared him for the shock. One-third of the Wa-

Wun catalogue drawer was filled with index cards listing various books about the Wall.

He went to the shelves in the History Department, and the formerly empty spaces were now filled with brightly bound new books printed on clean, glossy paper. Their title pages were all stamped, "Copyright, 1993."

There was no dust on any of them. Before he opened any of the pages he knew these books would contain only the sort of information "they" wanted him to believe. He read:

> In 1970, after the outbreak of the disastrous Intercontinental Atomic War which depopulated the world, construction of Wall-enclosed cities began. Thanks to the Wall, which is impervious to atomic attack or radiation, civilization has been permitted to survive. Today, in 1993, only a handful of Wall-enclosed cities remain to carry on man's struggle for self-preservation on a planet continually swept by atomic storms whose deadly fumes are held back only by the Wall—

Jim thought of the clean, fresh water that flowed from under the Wall, and put the book back on the shelf. Only the first book had told the truth. There had been no Atomic War and the Wall was not designed to keep poison fumes out, *but to keep him in Hillsboro*.

Why? There was no one that Jim could ask, for everyone was part of that indefinable, mysterious group which he could only call *they*. What was their purpose? Who was Jim Carrington that they should exert so much effort to keep him in ignorance? He thought he had enough evidence in the history book with which to confront them and demand an explanation, but Doc Barnes had taken it away from him. Very well, then, he would find additional proof, and when he confronted them with their lies, they would be forced to tell the truth.

That evening Doc Barnes came again to visit him. "Just thought I'd pass by," the doctor said as he sat down upon the porch rocking chair. "Hadn't seen you for some time. Been feeling all right?"

Jim nodded. "Funny thing," he said. "I had a queer dream about you last night."

Doc Barnes fanned himself. "Dreams have very little significance. I would just forget about it."

"Doc," Jim said slowly, "if I asked you an important question, would you give me an honest answer? You know that last night was no dream, and I know it. Would you answer just one question honestly?"

The doctor kept on fanning himself as he looked out across the field to where the stars could be seen through the invisible Wall.

"What's your question, Jim?" he asked, not turning to look into Jim's eyes.

"Tell me," Jim said, "am I—am I *different from everybody else?*"

The aurora borealis could be seen, its brilliant colors like some curtain hanging over Hillsboro. Both doctor and boy stared at it.

"Why do you ask?"

"'Cause I feel it."

Doc Barnes considered this and asked, with a strange note of regret in his voice, "You're not happy here?"

Jim shook his head, not daring to speak.

"Then what do you want?"

Jim pointed to the aurora whose vivid colors seemed to be draped somewhere halfway between the horizon and the dome of the never seen but always-sensed Wall.

"I want to go Outside," Jim said, knowing now what it was that had rankled within him for so many years. "I want to see what is on the other side of the Wall."

There was a sad expression on Doc Barnes' face, as if he knew what was there but could not voice his knowledge. It was not a thing that inspired fear or horror—as a world wracked with atomic poisons might—but something which was sad and lonely.

"I'm sorry," Doc Barnes said. There was nothing more to add, for in the doctor's inflection Jim could hear the refusal which *they* gave to his request for permission to leave Hillsboro.

"All right," Jim said, pretending to resign himself to the doctor's unwillingness to tell him the nature of the truth. He knew that if he were ever to learn the reason for the secrecy and deception he would find it only Outside—on the other side of the Wall.

When Doc Barnes had left and Jim was in bed, the plan slowly formed in his mind. The Carrington house was located on the outskirts of Hillsboro, only a few miles from the Wall itself. The aurora had died and there was no moon that night. He could reach the Wall within a few hours.

Jim crawled out of bed and dressed quickly and then climbed out of his window to step gingerly upon the porch. He jumped to the soft ground and then headed for the river. Despite the darkness he walked rapidly, and after three hours reached the point where the river flowed from underneath the Wall.

Jim stood on the brink for a moment, calculating the risks he took, and then plunged downward. He held his breath as he slid down against the glass-like substance of the Wall, his fingers clutching for the edge. He found it, gripped tight and pulled himself through against the rapid river current. Something slapped in his face, he kicked at the vague shadow in horror and then remembered that it might be a fish. His lungs now starved for precious air, he started to rise. If Doc Barnes and the history books were correct, he would die with the first breath when he reached the surface, and eventually they would find his corrupted body in the bed of the stream.

He kept on rising, and when his head broke the surface his lungs breathed in fresh, cool air. Pantingly he rested against the Wall, fighting the down-current that threatened to pull him back into Hillsboro. In the pitch darkness he could see nothing. After catching breath he pushed himself away from the Wall and swam towards where the river bank might be. His tired hands clutched at the shore, and he dragged himself upward and then rested upon the grassy bank.

While he lay there, breathing and waiting for the pounding of his heart to subside, he knew that the first step in his effort to find out the truth was successful. The Outside was not deadly. The air was fresh and clean, and nowhere around him could he see the atomic volcanoes that were said to throw their deadly missiles against the Wall. He had no equipment to measure radiation, but if there were no deadly fumes and he was still alive, he had a right to assume that the whole story was fictitious and there was no deadly radiation whatever.

It was too dark for Jim to see any part of the horizon. A glimmer of moonlight shot through the clouds, and for a moment Jim thought he saw a series of immense domes in the distance. The moon hid once more and again he was in total darkness. Placing his fingertips upon the Wall he cautiously walked forward and found himself upon some curving embankment that curled upward around the Wall. In place of steps there were a series of deep indentations which made it difficult for him to secure good footing. He found at eye level against the Wall a rail which served as a sort of guide. Using this he drew himself along.

When the moon broke through again he was astonished to see the entire town of Hillsboro stretched before him as a sort of huge diorama. He could see clearly every single house and street and the familiar woodlands where he had played as a boy.

The road on which Jim walked rose higher, still hugging the Wall, and he knew that while he could see through the Wall into Hillsboro, vision was possible only in this one direction. He had often stared through this same section of Wall and seen only a vague haze which everyone assured him was only mist or fog.

Hillsboro, from the height where he stood, did not look like New York or Moscow, or any of the other really big cities of the Earth which he had seen pictured in some of the older history books. Rather it had a bit of all of them, and he now understood who he was and why he was so important.

The truth became evident when he reached up about one fourth of the height of the ramp, and touched the first of three small projections beneath the rail.

As he did so a clear, sharp thought formed itself in his mind.
Species: Man.

He looked about him, thinking someone had spoken. He touched the first lever again. Once more the thought rang in his mind.
Species: Man.

This was some sort of telepathic communication, he realized, and then touched the second lever.

Habitat: Third Planet, Sun. Farm area in temperate zone of northern hemisphere.

Third lever.

Special Note: A remarkable feature of this unique exhibit is the actual presence of a living, warm-blooded, oxygen-breathing Man among the Robot-Duplicate models. For many centuries the Museum had attempted to maintain living colonies but all experiments had failed. As the Third Planet became settled by colonists from..., Man specimens became increasingly difficult to obtain. It is believed that Jim Carrington, as the Man Specimen contained in this exhibit is named, is the last of his species, his small tribe having annihilated itself rather than submit to taming by... scientists. Jim Carrington was brought to... and this model constructed by the Museum directors. It is complete with Robot-Duplicate models of all known types of Man Specimens. The extraordinary skill with which the exhibit was prepared is attested to by the fact that even at this moment the last living Man Specimen, Jim Carrington, is not aware of the true situation. The model you see is a typical Earth community as it existed two hundred years ago.

Jim Carrington knew who he was at last. There was a slithering motion on the ramp and he turned to face the Keeper of the Natural Habitat Zoo.

Before he saw the alien, a last furtive thought-message thrust itself upon his mind:

Caution! Do not feed or harbor escaped specimens. Deliver them immediately to the dissection chambers.

COMPUTERS DON'T ARGUE

Gordon R. Dickson

Books enrich our lives by providing us with knowledge; they can also be (like the book you have in your hands) very entertaining as well. They are almost never dangerous—unless they are supplied by a book club run by a computer like the one in this story. Computers may not argue, but the mistakes they make can mean serious trouble for mere humans.

TREASURE BOOK CLUB

PLEASE DO NOT FOLD,
SPINDLE OR MUTILATE
THIS CARD

Mr: Walter A. Child Balance: $4.98

Dear Customer: Enclosed is your latest book selection. "Kidnapped," by Robert Louis Stevenson.

Woodlawn Drive
Panduk, Michigan
Nov. 16, 1965

Treasure Book Club
1823 Mandy Street
Chicago, Illinois

Dear Sirs:

I wrote you recently about the computer punch card you sent, billing me for "Kim," by Rudyard Kipling. I did not open the package containing it until I had already mailed you my check for the amount on the card. On opening the package, I found the book missing half its pages. I sent it back to you, requesting either another copy or my money back. Instead, you have sent me a copy of "Kidnapped," by Robert Louis Stevenson. Will you please straighten this out?

I hereby return the copy of "Kidnapped."

Sincerely yours,
Walter A. Child

TREASURE BOOK CLUB

SECOND NOTICE
PLEASE DO NOT FOLD,
SPINDLE OR MUTILATE
THIS CARD

Mr: Walter A. Child Balance $4.98

For "Kidnapped," by Robert Louis Stevenson. (If remittance has been made for the above, please disregard this notice)

> 437 Woodlawn Drive
> Panduk, Michigan
> Jan. 21, 1966

Treasure Book Club
1823 Mandy Street
Chicago, Illinois

Dear Sirs:

May I direct your attention to my letter of November 16, 1965? You are still continuing to dun me with computer punch cards for a book I did not order. Whereas, actually, it is your company that owes *me* money.

> Sincerely yours,
> Walter A. Child

> Treasure Book Club
> 1823 Mandy Street
> Chicago, Illinois
> Feb. 1, 1966

Mr. Walter A. Child
437 Woodlawn Drive
Panduk, Michigan

Dear Mr. Child:

We have sent you a number of reminders concerning an amount owing to us as a result of book purchases you have made from us. This amount, which is $4.98, is now long overdue.

This situation is disappointing to us, particularly since there was no hesitation on our part in extending you credit at the time original arrangements for these purchases were made by you. If we do not receive payment in full by return mail, we will be forced to turn the matter over to a collection agency.

Very truly yours,
Samuel P. Grimes
Collection Mgr.

437 Woodlawn Drive
Panduk, Michigan
Feb. 5, 1966

Dear Mr. Grimes:

Will you stop sending me punch cards and form letters and make me some kind of a direct answer from a human being?

I don't owe you money. *You* owe me money. Maybe I should turn your company over to a collection agency.

Walter A. Child

FEDERAL COLLECTION
OUTFIT

88 Prince Street
Chicago, Illinois
Feb. 28, 1966

Mr. Walter A. Child
437 Woodlawn Drive
Panduk, Michigan

Dear Mr. Child:

Your account with the Treasure Book Club, of $4.98 plus interest and charges has been turned over to our agency for collection. The amount due is now $6.83. Please send your check for this amount or we shall be forced to take immediate action.

Jacob N. Harshe
Vice President

FEDERAL COLLECTION
OUTFIT

88 Prince Street
Chicago, Illinois
April 8, 1966

Mr. Walter A. Child
437 Woodlawn Drive
Panduk, Michigan

Dear Mr. Child:

You have seen fit to ignore our courteous requests to settle your long overdue account with Treasure Book Club, which is now, with accumulated interest and charges, in the amount of $7.51.

If payment in full is not forthcoming by April 11, 1966 we will be forced to turn the matter over to our attorneys for immediate court action.

Ezekiel B. Harshe
President

MALONEY, MAHONEY,
MACNAMARA and PRUITT
Attorneys

89 Prince Street
Chicago, Illinois
April 29, 1966

Mr. Walter A. Child
437 Woodlawn Drive
Panduk, Michigan

Dear Mr. Child:

Your indebtedness to the Treasure Book Club has been referred to us for legal action to collect.

This indebtedness is now in the amount of $10.01. If you will send us this amount so that we may receive it before May 5, 1966, the matter may be satisfied. However, if we do not receive satisfaction in full by that date, we will take steps to collect through the courts.

I am sure you will see the advantage of avoiding a judgment against you, which as a matter of record would do lasting harm to your credit rating.

Very truly yours,
Hagthorpe M. Pruitt Jr.
Attorney at law

437 Woodlawn Drive
Panduk, Michigan
May 4, 1966

Mr. Hagthorpe M. Pruitt, Jr.
Maloney, Mahoney, MacNamara and Pruitt
89 Prince Street
Chicago, Illinois

Dear Mr. Pruitt:

You don't know what a pleasure it is to me in this matter to get a letter from a live human being to whom I can explain the situation.

This whole matter is silly. I explained it fully in my letters to the Treasure Book Company. But I might as well have been trying to explain to the computer that puts out their punch cards, for all the good it seemed to do. Briefly, what happened was I ordered a copy of "Kim," by Rudyard Kipling, for $4.98. When I opened the package they sent me, I found the book had only half its pages, but I'd previously mailed a check to pay them for the book.

I sent the book back to them, asking either for a whole copy or my money back. Instead, they sent me a copy of "Kidnapped," by Robert Louis Stevenson—which I had not ordered; and for which they have been trying to collect from me.

Meanwhile, I am still waiting for the money back that they owe me for the copy of "Kim" that I didn't get. That's the whole story. Maybe you can help me straighten them out.

Relievedly yours,
Walter A. Child

P.S.: I also sent them back their copy of "Kidnapped," as soon as I got it, but it hasn't seemed to help. They have never even acknowledged getting it back.

MALONEY, MAHONEY,
MACNAMARA and PRUITT
Attorneys

89 Prince Street
Chicago, Illinois
May 9, 1966

Mr. Walter A. Child
437 Woodlawn Drive
Panduk, Michigan

Dear Mr. Child:

I am in possession of no information indicating that any item purchased by you from the Treasure Book Club has been returned.

I would hardly think that, if the case had been as you stated, the Treasure Book Club would have retained us to collect the amount owing from you.

If I do not receive your payment in full within three days, by May 12, 1966, we will be forced to take legal action.

Very truly yours,
Hagthorpe M. Pruitt Jr.

COURT OF MINOR CLAIMS
Chicago, Illinois

Mr. Walter A. Child   437 Woodlawn Drive   Panduk, Michigan

Be informed that a judgment was taken and entered against you in this court this day of May 26, 1966 in the amount of $15.66 including court costs.

Payment in satisfaction of this judgment may be made to this court or to the adjudged creditor. In the case of payment being made to the creditor, a release should be obtained from the creditor and filed with this court in order to free you of legal obligation in connection with this judgment.

Under the recent Reciprocal Claims Act, if you are a citizen of a different state, a duplicate claim may be automatically entered and judged against you in your own state so that collection may be made there as well as in the State of Illinois.

COURT OF MINOR CLAIMS
Chicago, Illinois

PLEASE DO NOT FOLD,
SPINDLE OR MUTILATE
THIS CARD

Judgment was passed this day of May 27, 1966, under Statute 15.66

> Against: Child, Walter A. of 437 Woodlawn Drive, Panduk, Michigan. Pray to enter a duplicate claim for judgment
> In: Picayune Court—Panduk, Michigan
> For Amount: Statute 941

437 Woodlawn Drive
Panduk, Michigan
May 31, 1966

Samuel P. Grimes
Vice President, Treasure Book Club
1823 Mandy Street
Chicago, Illinois

Grimes:

This business has gone far enough. I've got to come down to Chicago on business of my own tomorrow. I'll see you then and we'll get this straightened out once and for all, about who owes what to whom, and how much! Yours,
Walter A. Child

From the desk of the Clerk
Picayune Court

June 1, 1966

Harry:

The attached computer card from Chicago's Minor Claims Court against A. Walter has a 1500-series Statute number on it. That puts it over in Criminal with you, rather than Civil, with me. So I herewith submit it for your computer instead of mine. How's business? Joe

CRIMINAL RECORDS
Panduk, Michigan

PLEASE DO NOT FOLD,
SPINDLE OR MUTILATE
THIS CARD

Convicted: (Child) A. Walter

On: May 26, 1966

Address: 437 Woodlawn Drive, Panduk, Mich.

Crim: Statute: 1566 (Corrected) 1567

Crime: Kidnap

Date: Nov. 16, 1965

Notes: At large. To be picked up at once.

POLICE DEPARTMENT, PANDUK, MICHIGAN. TO POLICE DEPARTMENT CHI-CAGO, ILLINOIS. CONVICTED SUBJECT A. (COMPLETE FIRST NAME UN-KNOWN) WALTER, SOUGHT HERE IN CONNECTION REF. YOUR NOTIFICATION OF JUDGMENT FOR KIDNAP OF CHILD NAMED ROBERT LOUIS STEVENSON, ON NOV. 16, 1965. INFORMATION HERE INDICATES SUBJECT FLED HIS RESIDENCE, AT 437 WOODLAWN DRIVE, PANDUK, AND MAY AGAIN BE IN YOUR AREA.

POSSIBLE CONTACT IN YOUR AREA: THE TREASURE BOOK CLUB, 1823 MANDY STREET, CHICAGO, ILLINOIS. SUBJECT NOT KNOWN TO BE ARMED, BUT PRESUMED DANGEROUS. PICK UP AND HOLD, ADVISING US OF CAPTURE...

TO POLICE DEPARTMENT, PANDUK, MICHIGAN. REFERENCE YOUR RE-QUEST TO PICK UP AND HOLD A. (COMPLETE FIRST NAME UNKNOWN) WALTER, WANTED IN PANDUK ON STATUTE 1567, CRIME OF KIDNAPPING.

SUBJECT ARRESTED AT OFFICES OF TREASURE BOOK CLUB, OP-ERATING THERE UNDER ALIAS WALTER ANTHONY CHILD AND ATTEMPT-ING TO COLLECT $4.98 FROM ONE SAMUEL P. GRIMES, EMPLOYEE OF THAT COMPANY.

DISPOSAL: HOLDING FOR YOUR ADVICE.

POLICE DEPARTMENT PANDUK, MICHIGAN TO POLICE DEPARTMENT CHI-
CAGO, ILLINOIS.

REF: A. WALTER (ALIAS WALTER ANTHONY CHILD) SUBJECT WANTED
FOR CRIME OF KIDNAP, YOUR AREA, REF: YOUR COMPUTER PUNCH CARD
NOTIFICATION OF JUDGMENT, DATED MAY 27, 1966. COPY OUR CRIMINAL
RECORDS PUNCH CARD HEREWITH FORWARDED TO YOUR COMPUTER
SECTION.

CRIMINAL RECORDS
Chicago, Illinois

PLEASE DO NOT FOLD,
SPINDLE OR MUTILATE
THIS CARD

SUBJECT (CORRECTION—OMITTED RECORD SUPPLIED)
    APPLICABLE STATUTE NO. 1567
    JUDGMENT NO. 456789
    TRIAL RECORD: APPARENTLY MISFILED AND UNAVAILABLE
    DIRECTION: TO APPEAR FOR SENTENCING BEFORE JUDGE JOHN
ALEXANDER MCDIVOT, COURTROOM A JUNE 9, 1966

From the Desk of
JUDGE ALEXANDER J. McDIVOT

June 2, 1966

Dear Tony:
I've got an adjudged criminal coming up before me for sentencing
Thursday morning—but the trial transcript is apparently misfiled.

I need some kind of information (Ref: A. Walter—Judgment
No. 456789, Criminal). For example, what about the victim of the
kidnapping. Was victim harmed?   Jack McDivot

June 3, 1966

Records Search Unit
Re: Ref: Judgment No. 456789—was victim harmed?

Tonio Malagasi
Records Division

June 3, 1966

To: United States Statistics Office
Attn: Information Section
Subject: Robert Louis Stevenson
Query: Information concerning

Records Search Unit
Criminal Records Division
Police Department
Chicago, Ill.

June 5, 1966

To: Records Search Unit
Criminal Records Division
Police Department
Chicago, Illinois
Subject: Your query re Robert Louis Stevenson (File no. 189623)
Action: Subject deceased. Age at death, 44 yrs. Further information requested?   A. K.
Information Section
U. S. Statistics Office

June 6, 1966

To: United States Statistics Office
Attn.: Information Division
Subject: Re: File no. 189623
       No further information required.

Thank you.
Records Search Unit
Criminal Records Division
Police Department
Chicago, Illinois

June 7, 1966

To: Tonio Malagasi
Records Division
Re: Ref: judgment No. 456789—victim is dead.

Records Search Unit

June 7, 1966

To: Judge Alexander J. McDivot's Chambers

Dear Jack:

Ref: Judgment No. 456789. The victim in this kidnap case was apparently slain.

From the strange lack of background information on the killer and his victim, as well as the victim's age, this smells to me like a gangland killing. This for your information. Don't quote me. It seems to me, though, that Stevenson—the victim—has a name that rings a faint bell with me. Possibly, one of the East Coast Mob, since the association comes back to me as something about pirates—possibly New York dockage hijackers—and something about buried loot.

As I say, above is only speculation for your private guidance. Any time I can help...   Best,
                                                          Tony Malagasi
                                                          Records Division

MICHAEL R. REYNOLDS
Attorney-at-law

49 Water Street
Chicago, Illinois
June 8, 1966

Dear Tim:

Regrets: I can't make the fishing trip. I've been court-appointed here to represent a man about to be sentenced tomorrow on a kidnapping charge.

Ordinarily, I might have tried to beg off, and McDivot, who is doing the sentencing, would probably have turned me loose. But this is the damnedest thing you ever heard of.

The man being sentenced has apparently been not only charged, but adjudged guilty as a result of a comedy of errors too long to go into here. He not only isn't guilty—he's got the best case I ever heard of for damages against one of the larger Book Clubs headquartered here in Chicago. And that's a case I wouldn't mind taking on.

It's inconceivable—but damnably possible, once you stop to think of it in this day and age of machine-made records—that a completely innocent man could be put in this position.

There shouldn't be much to it. I've asked to see McDivot tomorrow before the time for sentencing, and it'll just be a matter of explaining to him. Then I can discuss the damage suit with my freed client at his leisure.

Fishing next weekend?

Yours,
Mike

MICHAEL R. REYNOLDS
Attorney-at-law

49 Water Street
Chicago, Illinois
June 10

Dear Tim:

In haste— No fishing this coming week either. Sorry.

You won't believe it. My innocent-as-a-lamb-and-I'm-not-kidding client has just been sentenced to death for first-degree murder in connection with the death of his kidnap victim.

Yes, I explained the whole thing to McDivot. And when he explained his situation to me, I nearly fell out of my chair.

It wasn't a matter of my not convincing him. It took less than three minutes to show him that my client should never have been within the walls of the County Jail for a second. But—get this— McDivot couldn't do a thing about it.

The point is, my man had already been judged guilty according to the computerized records. In the absence of a trial record—of course there never was one (but that's something I'm not free to explain to you now)—the judge has to go by what records are available. And in the case of an adjudged prisoner, McDivot's only legal choice was whether to sentence to life imprisonment, or execution.

The death of the kidnap victim, according to the statute, made the death penalty mandatory. Under the new laws governing length of time for appeal, which has been shortened because of the new system of computerizing records, to force an elimination of unfair delay and mental anguish to those condemned, I have five days in which to file an appeal, and ten to have it acted on.

Needless to say, I am not going to monkey with an appeal. I'm going directly to the Governor for a pardon—after which we will get this farce reversed. McDivot has already written the Governor, also, explaining that his sentence was ridiculous, but that he had no choice. Between the two of us, we ought to have a pardon in short order.

Then, I'll make the fur fly...
And we'll get in some fishing.

Best,
Mike

OFFICE OF THE GOVERNOR
OF ILLINOIS

June 17, 1966

Mr. Michael R. Reynolds
49 Water Street
Chicago, Illinois

Dear Mr. Reynolds:

In reply to your query about the request for pardon for Walter A. Child (A. Walter), may I inform you that the Governor is still on his trip with the Midwest Governors Committee, examining the Wall in Berlin. He should be back next Friday.

I will bring your request and letters to his attention the minute he returns.

Very truly yours,
Clara B. Jilks
Secretary to the Governor

June 27, 1966

Michael R. Reynolds
49 Water Street
Chicago, Illinois

Dear Mike:

Where is that pardon?
My execution date is only five days from now!

Walt

June 29, 1966

Walter A. Child (A. Walter)
Cell Block E
Illinois State Penitentiary
Joliet, Illinois

Dear Walt:

The Governor returned, but was called away immediately to the White House in Washington to give his views on interstate sewage.

I am camping on his doorstep and will be on him the moment he arrives here.

Meanwhile, I agree with you about the seriousness of the situation. The warden at the prison there, Mr. Allen Magruder, will bring this letter to you and have a private talk with you. I urge you to listen to what he has to say; and I enclose letters from your family also urging you to listen to Warden Magruder.

Yours,
Mike

June 30, 1966

Michael R. Reynolds
49 Water Street
Chicago, Illinois

Dear Mike: (This letter being smuggled out by Warden Magruder)

As I was talking to Warden Magruder in my cell, here, news was brought to him that the Governor has at last returned for a while to Illinois, and will be in his office early tomorrow morning, Friday. So you will have time to get the pardon signed by him and delivered to the prison in time to stop my execution on Saturday.

Accordingly, I have turned down the Warden's kind offer of a chance to escape; since he told me he could by no means guarantee to have all the guards out of my way when I tried it; and there was a chance of my being killed escaping.

But now everything will straighten itself out. Actually, an experience as fantastic as this had to break down sometime under its own weight.

Best,
Walt

FOR THE SOVEREIGN
STATE OF ILLINOIS

I, Hubert Daniel Willikens, Governor of the State of Illinois, and invested with the authority and powers appertaining thereto, including the power to pardon those in my judgment wrongfully convicted or otherwise deserving of executive mercy, do this day of July 1, 1966 announce and proclaim that Walter A. Child (A. Walter) now in custody as a consequence of erroneous conviction upon a crime of which he is entirely innocent, is fully and freely pardoned of said crime. And I do direct the necessary authorities having custody of the said Walter A. Child (A. Walter) in whatever place or places he may be held, to immediately free, release, and allow unhindered departure to him...

INTERDEPARTMENTAL
ROUTING SERVICE

PLEASE DO NOT FOLD,
SPINDLE OR MUTILATE,
THIS CARD

Failure to route Document properly.

To: Governor Hubert Daniel Willikens

Re: Pardon issued to Walter A. Child, July 1, 1966

Dear State Employee:
You have failed to attach your Routing Number.

PLEASE: Resubmit document with this card and form 876, explaining your authority for placing a TOP RUSH category on this document. Form 876 must be signed by your Departmental Superior.

RESUBMIT ON: Earliest possible date ROUTING SERVICE office is open. In this case, Tuesday, July 5, 1966.

WARNING: Failure to submit form 876 WITH THE SIGNATURE OF YOUR SUPERIOR may make you liable to prosecution for misusing a Service of the State Government. A warrant may be issued for your arrest.

There are NO exceptions. YOU have been WARNED.

PLACEMENT TEST

Keith Laumer

Sometimes, rules imposed from above seem incomprehensible and unfair. When those rules are imposed by government bureaucracies, they also seem impossible to fight. Keith Laumer, who once served his country as a foreign service officer, had to deal with such bureaucracies, and in this amusing story he tells us what he really thinks about them.

1

Reading the paper in his hand, Mart Maldon felt his mouth go dry. Across the desk, Dean Wormwell's eyes, blurry behind thick contact lenses, strayed to his fingerwatch.

"Quota'd out?" Maldon's voice emerged as a squeak. "Three days before graduation?"

"Umm, yes, Mr. Maldon. Pity, but there you are..." Wormwell's jowls twitched upward briefly. "No reflection on you, of course..."

Maldon found his voice. "They can't do this to me—I stand number two in my class—"

Wormwell held up a pudgy palm. "Personal considerations are not involved, Mr. Maldon. Student load is based on quarterly allocated funding; funds were cut. Analogy Theory was one of the courses receiving a quota reduction—"

"An Theory...? But I'm a Microtronics major; that's an elective—an optional one-hour course—"

The Dean rose, stood with his fingertips on the desk. "The details are there, in the notification letter—"

"What about the detail that I waited four years for enrollment, and I've worked like a malemute for five more—"

"Mr. Maldon!" Wormwell's eyes bulged. "We work within a system! You don't expect *personal* exceptions to be made, I trust?"

"But, Dean—there's a howling need for qualified Microtronic Engineers—"

"That will do, Mr. Maldon. Turn in your student tag to the Registrar and you'll receive an appointment for Placement Testing."

"All right," Maldon's chair banged as he stood up. "I can still pass Testing and get Placed; I know as much Micro as any graduate—"

"Ah—I believe you're forgetting the limitation on nonacademically qualified testees in Technical Specialty Testing. I suggest you accept a Phase Two Placement for the present..."

"Phase Two—But that's for unskilled labor!"

"You need work, Mr. Maldon. A city of a hundred million can't support idlers. And dormitory life is far from pleasant for an untagged man." The Dean waited, glancing pointedly at the door. Maldon silently gathered up his letter and left.

2

It was hot in the test cubicle. Maldon shifted on the thinly added bench, looking over the test form:

1. In the following list of words, which word is repeated most often: dog, cat, cow, cat, pig...

2. Would you like to ask persons entering a building to show you their pass?

3. Would you like to check forms to see if the names have been entered in the correct space?

"Testing materials are on the desk," a wall-speaker said. "Use the stylus to mark the answers you think are correct. Mark only one answer to each question. You will have one hour in which to complete the test. You may start now..."

Back in the Hall twenty minutes later, Maldon took a seat on a bench against the wall beside a heavy-faced man who sat with one hand clutching the other as though holding a captured mouse. Opposite him, a nervous youth in issue coveralls shook a cigaret from a crumpled plastic pack lettered GRANYAUCK WELFARE— ONE DAILY RATION, puffed it alight, exhaled an acrid whiff of combustion retardant.

"That's a real smoke," he said in a high, rapid voice, rolling the thin, greyish cylinder between his fingers. "Half an inch of doctored tobacco and an inch and a half of filter." He grinned sourly and dropped the cigaret on the floor between his feet.

The heavy-faced man moved his head half an inch.

"That's safety first, Mac. Guys like you throw 'em around, they burn down and go out by theirself."

"Sure—if they'd make 'em half an inch shorter you could throw 'em away without lighting 'em at all."

Across the room a small man with jug ears moved along, glancing at the yellow or pink cards in the hands of the waiting men and women. He stopped, plucked a card from the hand of a narrow-faced boy with an open mouth showing crowded yellow teeth.

"You've already *passed,*" the little man said irritably. "You don't come back here anymore. Take the card and go to the place that's written on it. Here..." he pointed.

"Sixteen years I'm foreman of number nine gang-lathe at Philly Maintenance," the man sitting beside Mart said suddenly. He unfolded his hands, held out the right one. The tips of all four fingers were missing to the first knuckle. He put the hand away.

"When I get out of the Medicare, they classify me J-4 and send me here. And you know what?" He looked at Mart. "I can't pass the tests..."

"Maldon, Mart," an amplified voice said. "Report to the Monitor's desk..."

He walked across to the corner where the small man sat now, deftly sorting cards. He looked up, pinched a pink card from the stack, jabbed it at Maldon. Words jumped out at him: NOT QUALIFIED.

Mart tossed the card back on the desk. "You must be mixed up," he said. "A ten year old kid could pass that test—"

"Maybe so," the monitor said sharply. "But you didn't. Next testing on Wednesday, eight A. M.—"

"Hold on a minute," Mart said. "I've had five years of Microtronics—"

The monitor was nodding. "Sure, sure. Come back Wednesday."

"You don't get the idea—"

"You're the one that doesn't get the idea, fellow." He studied Maldon for a moment. "Look," he said, in a more reasonable tone. "What you want, you want to go in for Adjustment."

"Thanks for the tip," Maldon said. "I'm not quite ready to have my brains scrambled."

"Ha! A smart-alec!" The monitor pointed to his chest. "Do I look like my brains were scrambled?"

Maldon looked him over as though in doubt.

"You've been Adjusted, huh? What's it like?"

"Adjustment? There's nothing to it. You have a problem finding work, it helps you, that's all. I've seen fellows like you before. You'll never pass Phase Two testing until you do it."

"To Hell with Phase Two testing. I've registered for Tech Testing. I'll just wait."

The monitor nodded, prodding at his teeth with a pencil.

"Yeah, you could wait. I remember one guy waited nine years; then got his Adjustment and we placed him in a week."

"Nine years?" Maldon shook his head. "Who makes up these rules?"

"Who makes 'em up? Nobody! They're in the book."

Maldon leaned on the desk. "Then who writes the book? Where do I find them?"

"You mean the Chief?" the small man rolled his eyes toward the ceiling. "On the next level up. But don't waste your time, friend. You can't get in there. They don't have time to argue with everybody who comes in here. It's the system—"

"Yeah," Maldon said, turning away. "So I hear."

3

Maldoh rode the elevator up one floor, stepped off in a blank-walled foyer, adorned by a stone urn filled with sand, a potted yucca, framed unit citations and a polished slab door lettered PLACEMENT BOARD—AUTHORIZED PERSONNEL ONLY. He tried it, found it solidly locked.

It was very quiet. Somewhere, air pumps hummed. Maldon stood by the door and waited. After ten minutes, the elevator door hissed open, disgorged a slow-moving man in blue GS coveralls with a yellow identity tag. He held the tag to a two-inch rectangle of glass beside the door. There was a click. The door slid back. Maldon moved quickly, crowding through behind the workman.

"Hey, what gives," the man said.

"It's all right, I'm a coordinator," Maldon said quickly.

"Oh." The man looked Maldon over. "Hey," he said. "Where's your I.D.?"

"It's a new experimental system. It's tattooed on my left foot."

"Hah!" the man said. "They always got to try out new stuff." He went on along the deep-carpeted corridor. Maldon followed slowly, reading signs over doors. He turned in under one that read CRITERIA SECTION. A girl with features compressed by fat looked up, her lower jaw working busily. She reached, pressed a button on the desk top.

"Hi," Maldon said, using a large smile. "I'd like to see the chief of the section."

The girl chewed, looking at him.

"I won't take up much of his time..."

"You sure won't, Buster," the girl said. The hall door opened. A uniformed man looked in. The girl waved a thumb at Maldon.

"He comes busting in," she said. "No tag, yet." The guard jerked his head toward the corridor. "Let's go..."

"Look, I've got to see the chief—"

The cop took his arm, helped him to the door. "You birds give me a swifty. Why don't you go to Placement like the sign says?"

"Look, they tell me I've got to have some kind of electronic lobotomy to make me dumb enough to be a receptionist or a watchman—"

"Let's watch them cracks," the guard said. He shoved Maldon out into the waiting room. "Out! And don't pull any more fasties until you got a tag, see?"

4

Sitting at a shiny imitation-oak table in the Public Library, Mart turned the pages of a booklet titled *Adjustment Fits the Man to the Job*.

"...neuroses arising from job tension," he read at random. "Thus, the Adjusted worker enjoys the deep-down satisfaction which comes from Doing a Job, free from conflict-inducing non-productive impulses and the distractions of feckless speculative intellectual activity..."

Mart rose and went to the librarian's console.

"I want something a little more objective," he said in a hoarse library whisper. "This is nothing but propaganda."

The librarian paused in her button-punching to peer at the booklet. "That's put out by the Placement people themselves," she said sharply. She was a jawless woman with a green tag against a ribby chest and thin, black-dyed hair. "It contains all the information anyone needs."

"Not quite; it doesn't tell who grades Placement tests and decides who gets their brain poached."

"Well!" the woman's button chin drew in. "I'm sure I never heard Adjustment referred to in *those* terms before!"

"Do you have any technical information on it—or anything on Placement policy in general?"

"Certainly not for indiscriminate use by—" she searched for a word, "—browsers!"

"Look, I've got a right to know what goes on in my own town, I hope," Mart said, forgetting to whisper. "What is it, a conspiracy...?"

"You're paranoid!" The librarian's lean fingers snatched the pamphlet from Maldon's hand. "You're all alike! You come stamping in here—without even a tag—a great healthy creature like you—" her voice cut like a sheet-metal file. Heads turned. "You're a troublemaker."

"All I want is information—"

"—living in luxury on MY tax money! You ought to be—"

5

It was an hour later. In a ninth-floor corridor of the GRAN-YAUCK TIMES HERALD building, Mart leaned against a wall, mentally rehearsing speeches. A stout man emerged from a door lettered EDITOR IN CHIEF. Mart stepped forward to intercept him.

"Pardon me, sir. I have to see you..."

Sharp blue eyes under wild-growing brows darted at Maldon. "Yes? What is it?"

"I have a story for you. It's about the Placement procedure."

"Whoa, buddy. Who are you?"

"My name's Maldon. I'm an Applied Tech graduate—almost—but I can't get placed in Microtronics. I don't have a tag—and the only way to get one is to get a job—but first I have to let the government operate on my brains—"

"Hmmmp!" The man looked Maldon up and down, started on.

"Listen!" Maldon caught at the portly man's arm. "They're making idiots out of intelligent people so they can do work you could train a chimp to do, and if you ask any questions—"

"All right, Mac..." A voice behind Maldon growled. A large hand took him by the shoulder, propelled him toward the walkaway entrance, urged him through the door. He straightened his coat, looked back. A heavy-set man with a pink card in a plastic cover clipped to his collar dusted his hands, looking satisfied.

"Don't come around lots," he called cheerfully as the door slammed.

6

"Hi Glamis," Mart said to the small, neat woman behind the small, neat desk. She smiled nervously, straightened the mathematically precise stack of papers before her.

"Mart, it's lovely to see you again, of course..." her eyes went to the blank place where his tag should have been. "But you really should have gone to your assigned SocAd Advisor—"

"I couldn't get an appointment until January." He pulled a chair around to the desk and sat down. "I've left school. I went in for Phase Two Placement testing this morning. I flunked."

"Oh...I'm so sorry, Mart." She arranged a small smile on her face. "But you can go back on Wednesday—"

"Uh-huh. And then on Friday, and then the following Monday—"

"Why, Mart, I'm sure you'll do better next time," the girl said brightly. She flipped through the pages of a calendar pad. "Wednesday's testing is for...ah...Vehicle Positioning Specialists, Instrumentation Inspectors, Sanitary Facility Supervisors—"

"Uh-huh. Toilet Attendants," Mart said. "Meter Readers—"

"There are others," Glamis went on hastily. "Traffic flow coordinators—"

"Pushing stop-light buttons on the turnpike. But it doesn't matter what the job titles are. I can't pass the tests."

"Why, Mart...Whatever do you mean?"

"I mean that to get the kind of jobs that are open you have to be a nice, steady moron. And if you don't happen to qualify as such, they're prepared to make you into one."

"Mart, you're exaggerating! The treatment merely slows the synaptic response time slightly—and its effects can be reversed at any time. People of exceptional qualities are needed to handle the type work—"

"How can I fake the test results, Glamis? I need a job—unless I want to get used to Welfare coveralls and two T rations a day."

"Mart! I'm shocked that you'd suggest such a thing! Not that it would work. You can't fool the Board that easily—"

"Then fix it so I go in for Tech testing; you know I can pass."

She shook her head. "Heavens, Mart, Tech Testing is all done at Central Personnel in City Tower—Level Fifty. Nobody goes up there, without at least a blue tag—" She frowned sympathetically. "You should simply have your adjustment, and—"

Maldon looked surprised. "You really expect me to go down there and have them cut my I. Q. down to 80 so I can get a job shovelling garbage?"

"Really, Mart; you can't expect society to adjust to *you.* You have to adjust to it."

"Look, I can punch commuters' tickets just as well as if I were stupid. I could—"

Glamis shook her head. "No, you couldn't, Mart. The Board knows what it's doing." She lowered her voice. "I'll be perfectly frank with you. These jobs *MUST* be filled. But they can't afford to put perceptive, active minds on rote tasks. There'd only be trouble. They need people who'll be contented and happy punching tickets."

Mart sat pulling at his lower lip. "All right, Glamis. Maybe I will go in for Adjustment..."

"Oh, wonderful, Mart." She smiled. "I'm *sure* you'll be happier—"

"But first, I want to know more about it. I want to be sure they aren't going to make a permanent idiot out of me."

She tsked, handed over a small folder from a pile on the corner of the desk.

"This will tell you—"

He shook his head. "I saw that. It's just a throwaway for the public. I want to know how the thing works; circuit diagrams, technical specs."

"Why, Mart, I don't have anything of that sort—and even if I did—"

"You can get 'em. I'll wait."

"Mart, I *do* want to help you...but...what...?"

"I'm not going in for Adjustment until I know something about it," he said flatly. "I want to put my mind at ease that they're not going to burn out my cortex."

Glamis nibbled her upper lip. "Perhaps I *could* get something from Central Files." She stood. "Wait here; I won't be long."

She was back in five minutes carrying a thick book with a cover of heavy manila stock on which were the words, *GSM 8765-89. Operation and Maintenance, EET Mark II.* Underneath, in smaller print, was a notice:

This Field Manual for Use of Authorized Personnel Only.

"Thanks, Glamis." Mart riffled the pages, glimpsed fine print and intricate diagrams. "I'll bring it back tomorrow." He headed for the door.

"Oh, you can't take it out of the office! You're not even *supposed* to *look* at it!"

"You'll get it back." He winked and closed the door on her worried voice.

7

The cubicle reminded Mart of the one at the Placement center, three days earlier, except that it contained a high, narrow cot in place of a desk and chair. A damp-looking attendant in a white coat flipped a wall switch, twiddled a dial.

"Strip to your waist, place your clothing and shoes in the basket, remove all metal objects from your pockets, no watches or other jewelry must be worn," he recited in a rapid monotone. "When you are ready, lie down on your back—" he slapped the cot— "hands at your sides, breathe deeply, do not touch any of the equipment. I will return in approximately five minutes. Do not leave the stall." He whisked the curtain aside and was gone.

Mart slipped a flat plastic tool kit from his pocket, opened it out, picked the largest screwdriver, and went to work on the metal panel cover set against the wall. He lifted it off and looked in at a maze of junction blocks, vari-colored wires, bright screwheads, fuses, tiny condensers.

He pulled a scrap of paper from his pocket, compared it to the circuits before him. The large black lead, here...He put a finger on it. And the matching red one, leading up from the 30 MFD condenser...

With a twist, he freed the two connectors, reversed them, tightened them back in place. Working quickly, he snipped wires, fitted jumpers in place, added a massive resistor from his pocket. There; with luck, the check instruments would give the proper readings now—but the current designed to lightly scorch his synapses would flow harmlessly round and round within the apparatus.

He clapped the cover back in place, screwed it down, and had just pulled off his shirt when the attendant thrust his head inside the curtains.

"Let's go, let's get those clothes off and get on the cot," he said, and disappeared.

Maldon emptied his pockets, pulled off his shoes, stretched out on the cot. A minute or two ticked past. There was an odor of alcohol in the air. The curtain jumped aside. The round-faced attendant took his left arm, swiped a cold tuft of cotton across it, held a hypo-spray an inch from the skin, and depressed the plunger. Mart felt a momentary sting.

"You've been given a harmless soporific," the attendant said tonelessly. "Just relax, don't attempt to change the position of the headset or chest contacts after I have placed them in position, are you beginning to feel drowsy...?"

Mart nodded. A tingling had begun in his fingertips; his head seemed to be inflating slowly. There was a touch of something cold across his wrists, then his ankles, pressure against his chest...

"Do not be alarmed, the restraint is for your own protection, relax and breathe deeply, it will hasten the effects of the soporific..." The voice echoed, fading and swelling. For a moment, the panicky thought came to Mart that perhaps he had made a mistake, that the modified apparatus would send a lethal charge through his brain... Then that thought was gone with all the others, lost in a swirling as of a soft green mist.

8

He was sitting on the side of the cot, and the attendant was offering him a small plastic cup. He took it, tasted the sweet liquid, handed it back.

"You should drink this," the attendant said, "It's very good for you."

Mart ignored him. He was still alive; and the attendant appeared to have noticed nothing unusual. So far, so good. He glanced at his hand. *One, two, three, four, five...* He could still count. *My name is Mart Maldon, age twenty-eight, place of residence, Welfare Dorm 69, Wing Two, nineteenth floor, room 1906...*

His memory seemed to be OK. *Twenty-seven times eighteen is...four hundred and eighty-six...*

He could still do simple arithmetic.

"Come on, fellow, drink the nice cup, then put your clothes on."

He shook his head, reached for his shirt, then remembered to move slowly, uncertainly, like a moron ought to. He fumbled clumsily with his shirt...

The attendant muttered, put the cup down, snatched the shirt, helped Mart into it, buttoned it for him.

"Put your stuff in your pockets, come on, that's a good fellow..."

He allowed himself to be led along the corridor, smiling

vaguely at people hurrying past. In the processing room, a starched woman back of a small desk stamped papers, took his hand and impressed his thumbprint on them, slid them across the desk.

"Sign your name here..." she pointed. Maldon stood gaping at the paper. There was absolutely no sign of comprehension.

"Write your name here!" She tapped the paper impatiently. Maldon reached up and wiped his nose with a forefinger, letting his mouth hang open.

The woman looked past him. "A Nine-oh-one," she snapped. "We can't be bothered. Take him back—"

Maldon grabbed the pen and wrote his name in large, scrawling letters. The woman snapped the form apart, thrust one sheet at him.

"Uh, I was thinking," he explained, folding the paper clumsily.

"Next!" the woman snapped, waving him on. He nodded submissively and shuffled slowly to the door.

9

The Placement monitor looked at the form Maldon had given him. He looked up, smiling. "Well, so you finally wised up. Good boy. And today you got a nice score. We're going to be able to place you. You like bridges, hah?"

Maldon hesitated, then nodded.

"Sure you like bridges. Out in the open air. You're going to be an important man. When the cars come up, you lean out and see that they put the money in the box. You get to wear a uniform..." The small man rambled on, filling out forms. Maldon stood by, looking at nothing.

"Here you go. Now, you go where it says right here, see? Just get on the cross-town shuttle, right outside on this level, the one with the big number nine. You know what a nine is, OK?"

Maldon blinked, nodded. The clerk frowned. "Sometimes I think them guys overdo a good thing. But you'll get to feeling better in a few days; you'll sharpen up, like me. Now, you go on over there, and they'll give you your I.D. and your uniform and put you to work. OK?"

"Uh, thanks..." Maldon crossed the wide room, pushed

through the turnstile, emerged into the late-afternoon sunlight on the fourth-level walkaway. The glare panel by the shuttle entrance read NEXT—9. He thrust his papers into his pocket and ran for it.

10

Maldon left his Dormitory promptly at eight the next morning, dressed in his threadbare Student-issue suit, carrying the heavy duffel-bag of Port Authority uniforms which had been issued to him the day before. His new yellow tag was pinned prominently to his lapel.

He took a cargo car to street level, caught an uptown car, dropped off in the run-down neighborhood of second-hand stores centered around Fifth Avenue and Forty-fifth Street. He picked a shabby establishment barricaded behind racks of dowdy garments, stepped into a long, dim-lit room smelling of naphtha and mouldy wool. Behind a counter, a short man with a circlet of fuzz above his ears and a vest hanging open over a tight-belted paunch looked him over. Mart hoisted the bag up, opened it, dumped the clothing out onto the counter. The paunchy man followed the action with his eyes.

"What'll you give me for this stuff?" Mart said.

The man behind the counter prodded the dark blue tunic, put a finger under the light blue trousers, rubbed the cloth. He leaned across the counter, glanced toward the door, squinted at Mart's badge. His eyes flicked to Mart's face, back to the clothing. He spread his hands.

"Five credits."

"For all of it? It's worth a hundred anyway."

The man glanced sharply at Maldon's face, back at his tag, frowning.

"Don't let the tag throw you," Maldon said. "It's stolen—just like the rest of the stuff."

"Hey." The paunchy man thrust his lips out. "What kinda talk is that? I run a respectable joint. What are you, some kinda cop?"

"I haven't got any time to waste," Maldon said. "There's nobody listening. Let's get down to business. You can strip off the braid and buttons and—"

"Ten credits, my top offer," the man said in a low voice. "I gotta stay alive, ain't I? Any bum can get outfitted free at the Welfare; who's buying my stuff?"

"I don't know. Make it twenty."

"Fifteen; it's robbery."

"Throw in a set of Maintenance coveralls, and it's a deal."

"I ain't got the real article, but close..."

Ten minutes later, Mart left the store wearing a grease-stained coverall with the cuffs turned up, the yellow tag clipped to the breast pocket.

11

The girl at the bleached-driftwood desk placed austerely at the exact center of the quarter-acre of fog-grey rug stared at Maldon distastefully.

"I know of no trouble with the equipment—" she started in a lofty tone.

"Look, sister, I'm in the plumbing line; you run your dictyper." Maldon swung a greasy tool box around by the leather strap as though he were about to lower it to the rug. "They tell me the Exec gym, Level 9, City Tower, that's where I go. Now, you want to tell me where the steam room is, or do I go back and file a beef with the Union...?"

"Next time come up the service shaft, Clyde!" she jabbed at a button; a panel whooshed aside across the room. "Men to the right, women to the left, co-ed straight ahead. Take your choice."

He went along the tiled corridor, passed steam-frosted doors. The passage turned right, angled left again. Mart pushed through a door, looked around at chromium and red plastic benches, horses, parallel bars, racks of graduated weights. A fat man in white shorts lay on the floor, halfheartedly pedaling his feet in the air. Mart crossed the room, tried another door.

Warm, sun-colored light streamed through an obscure-glass ceiling. Tropical plants in tubs nodded wide leaves over a mat of grass-green carpet edging a turquoise-tiled pool with chrome railings. Two brown-skinned men in brief trunks and sun-glasses sprawled on inflated rafts. There was a door to the right lettered

EXECUTIVE DRESSING ROOM—MEMBERS ONLY. Mart went to it, stepped inside.

Tall, ivory-colored lockers lined two walls, with a wide, padded bench between them. Beyond, bright shower heads winked in a darkened shower room. Maldon put the tool box on the bench, opened it, took out a twelve-inch prybar, looked around at the lockers. A monogrammed cigaret butt lay on the floor before one; he tried it first.

By levering at the top of the tall locker door, he was able to bulge it out sufficiently to see the long metal strip on the back of the door which secured it. He went back to the tool box, picked out a slim pair of pincers; with them he gripped the locking strip, levered up; the door opened with a sudden clang. The locker was empty.

He tried the next; it contained a handsome pale tan suit which would have fitted him nicely at the age of twelve. He went to the next locker...

Four lockers later, a door popped open on a dark maroon suit of expensive-looking polyon, a pair of plain scarlet shoes, a crisp pink shirt. Mart checked quickly. There was a wallet stuffed with ten-credit notes, a club membership card, and a blue I.D. with a gold alligator clip. Mart left the money on the shelf, rolled the clothing and stuffed it into the tool box, made for the door. It swung open and the smaller of the two sun bathers pushed past him with a sharp glance. Mart walked quickly around the end of the pool, stepped into the corridor. At the far end of it, the girl from the desk stood talking emphatically to a surprised-looking man. Their eyes turned toward Mart. He pushed through the first door on the left into a room with a row of white-sheeted tables, standing lamps with wide reflectors, an array of belted and rollered equipment. A vast bulk of a man with hairy forearms and a bald head, wearing tight white leotards and white sneakers folded a newspaper and looked up from his bench, wobbling a toothpick in the corner of his mouth. There was a pink tag on his chest.

"Uh...showers?" Mart inquired. The fat man nodded toward a door behind him. Mart stepped to it, found himself in a long room studded with showerheads and control knobs. There was no other door out. He turned back, bumped into the fat man in the doorway.

"So somebody finally decided to do something about the leak," he said around the toothpick. "Three months since I phoned it in. You guys take your time, hah?"

"I've got to go back for my tools," Mart said, starting past him. The fat man blocked him without moving. "So what's in the box?"

"Ah, they're the wrong tools..." He tried to sidle past. The big man took the toothpick from his mouth, frowned at it.

"You got a pipe wrench, ain't you? You got crescents, a screwdriver. What else you need to fix a lousy leak?"

"Well, I need my sprog-depressor," Mart said, "and my destrafficator rings, and possibly a marpilizer or two..."

"How come you ain't got—what you said—in there." The fat man eyed the tool box. "Ain't that standard equipment?"

"Yes, indeed—but I only have a right-hand one, and—"

"Let's have a look—" A fat hand reached for the tool-kit. Mart backed.

"—but I might be able to make it work," he finished. He glanced around the room. "Which one was it?"

"That third needle-battery on the right. You can see the drip. I'm tryna read, it drives me nuts."

Mart put the tool-box down. "If you don't mind, it makes me nervous to work in front of an audience..."

The fat man grunted and withdrew. Mart opened the box, took out a wrench, began loosening a wide hex-sided locking ring. Water began to dribble, then spurt. Mart went to the door, flung it open.

"Hey, you didn't tell me the water wasn't turned off..."

"Huh?"

"You'll have to turn off the master valve; hurry up, before the place is flooded!"

The fat man jumped up, headed for the door.

"Stand by it, wait five minutes, then turn it back on!" Mart called after him. The door banged. Mart hauled the tool-box out into the massage room, quickly stripped off the grimy coverall. His eye fell on a rack of neatly-packaged underwear, socks, toothbrushes, combs. He helped himself to a set, removed the last of the Welfare issue clothing—

A shout sounded outside the door, running feet. The door burst open.

"Where's Charlie? Some rascal's stolen my clothing...!"

Mart grabbed up a towel, dropped it over his head and rubbed vigorously, humming loudly, his back to the newcomer.

"The workman—there's his tool-box!"

Mart whirled, pulled the towel free, snatched the box from the hand of the invader, with a hearty shove sent him reeling into the locker room. He slammed the door, turned the key and dropped it down a drain. The shouts from inside were barely audible. He wrapped the towel around himself and dashed into the hall. There were people, some in white, others in towels or street clothes, all talking at once.

"Down there!" Mart shouted, pointing vaguely. "Don't let him get away!" He plunged through the press, along the hall. Doors opened and shut.

"Hey, what's he doing with a tool-box?" someone shouted. Mart whirled, dived through a door, found himself in a dense, hot fog. A woman with pink skin beaded with perspiration and a towel wrapped turban-fashion around her head stared at him.

"What are you doing in here? Co-ed is the next room along."

Mart gulped and dived past her, slammed through a plain door, found himself in a small room stacked with cartons. There was another door in the opposite wall. He went through it, emerged in a dusty hall. Three doors down, he found an empty store-room.

Five minutes later he emerged, dressed in a handsome maroon suit. He strode briskly along to a door marked EXIT, came out into a carpeted foyer with a rank of open elevator doors. He stepped into one. The yellow-tagged attendant whooshed the door shut.

"Tag, sir?" Maldon showed the blue I. D. The operator nodded.

"Down, sir?"

"No," Mart said. "Up."

12

He stepped out into the cool silence of Level Fifty.

"Which way to the Class One Testing Rooms?" he asked briskly.

The operator pointed. The door-lined corridor seemed to stretch endlessly.

"Going to try for the Big One, eh, sir?" the operator said. "Boy, you couldn't hire me to take on them kind of jobs. Me, I wouldn't want the responsibility." The closing door cut off the view of his wagging head.

Maldon set off, trying to look purposeful. Somewhere on this level were the Central Personnel Files, according to Glamis. It shouldn't be too hard to find them. After that... well, he could play it by ear.

A menu-board directory at a cross-corridor a hundred yards from his starting-point indicated PERSONNEL ANALYSIS to the right. Mart followed the passage, passed open doors through which he caught glimpses of soft colors, air-conditioner grills, potted plants, and immaculate young women with precise hair styles sitting before immense key boards or behind bare desks. Chaste lettering on doors read PROGRAMMING; REQUIREMENTS; DATA EXTRAPOLATION—PHASE III...

Ahead, Maldon heard a clattering, rising in volume as he approached a wide double door. He peered through glass, saw a long room crowded with massive metal cases ranked in rows, floor to ceiling. Men in tan dust smocks moved in the aisles, referring to papers in their hands, jotting notes, punching keys set in the consoles spaced at intervals on the giant cabinets. At a desk near the door, a man with a wide, sad mouth and a worried expression looked up, caught sight of Mart. It was no time to hesitate. He pushed through the door.

"Morning," he said genially over the busy sound of the data machines. "I'm looking for Central Personnel. I wonder if I'm in the right place?"

The sad man opened his mouth, then closed it. He had a green tag attached to the collar of his open-necked shirt.

"You from Special Actions?" he said doubtfully.

"Aptical foddering," Maldon said pleasantly. "I'd never been over here in Personnel Analysis, so I said, what the heck, I'll just run over myself." He was holding a relaxed smile in place, modelled after the one Dean Wormwell had customarily worn when condescending to students.

"Well, sir, this is Data Processing; what you probably want is Files..."

Mart considered quickly. "Just what is the scope of the work you do here?"

The clerk got to his feet. "We maintain the Master Personnel Cards up-to-date," he started, then paused. "Uh, could I just see that I. D., sir?"

Maldon let the smile cool a degree or two, flashed the blue card; the clerk craned as Mart tucked the tag away.

"Now," Mart went on briskly, "Suppose you just start at the beginning and give me a rundown." He glanced at a wall clock. "Make it a fast briefing. I'm a little pressed for time."

The clerk hitched at his belt, looked around. "Well, sir, let's start over here...

Ten minutes later, they stood before a high, glass-fronted housing inside which row on row of tape reels nestled on shiny rods; bright-colored plastic fittings of complex shape jammed the space over, under and behind each row.

"...it's all completely cybernetic-governed, of course," the clerk was saying. "We process an average of four hundred and nineteen thousand personnel actions per day, with an average relay-delay of not over four micro-seconds."

"What's the source of your input?" Mart inquired in the tone of one dutifully asking the routine questions.

"All the Directorates feed their data in to us—"

"Placement Testing?" Mart asked idly.

"Oh, sure, that's our biggest single data input."

"Including Class Five and Seven categories, for example?"

The clerk nodded. "Eight through Two. Your Tech categories are handled separately, over in Banks Y and X. There..." He pointed to a pair of red-painted cabinets.

"I see. That's where the new graduates from the Technical Institutions are listed, eh?"

"Right, sir. They're scheduled out from there to Testing alphabetically, and then ranked by score for Grading, Classification, and Placement."

Mart nodded and moved along the aisle. There were two-inch high letters stencilled on the frames of the data cases. He stopped before a large letter B.

"Let's look at a typical record," Mart suggested. The clerk stepped to the console, pressed a button. A foot-square screen glowed. Print popped into focus on it: BAJUL, FELIX B. 654-8734-099-B1/age 37....

Below the heading was an intricate pattern of dots.

"May I?" Mart reached for the button, pushed it. There was a click and the name changed: BAKARSKI, HYMAN A.

He looked at the meaningless code under the name.

"I take it each dot has a significance?"

"In the first row, you have the physical profile; that's the first nine spaces. Then psych, that's the next twenty-one. Then..." He lectured on. Mart nodded.

"...educational profile, right here..."

"Now," Mart cut in. "Suppose there were an error—say in the median scores attained by an individual. How could you correct that?"

The clerk frowned, pulling down the corners of his mouth into well-worn grooves.

"I don't mean on your part, of course," Mart said hastily. "But I imagine that the data processing equipment occasionally drops a decimal, eh?" He smiled understandingly.

"Well, we do get maybe one or two a year—but there's no harm done. On the next run-through, the card's automatically kicked out."

"So you don't...ah...make corrections?"

"Well, only when a Change Entry comes through."

The clerk twirled knobs; the card moved aside, up; a single dot swelled on the screen, resolved into a pattern of dots.

"Say it was on this item; I'd just wipe that code, and overprint the change. Only takes a second, and—"

"Suppose, for example, you wanted this record corrected to show graduation from a Tech Institute?"

"Well, that would be this symbol here; eighth row, fourth entry. The code for technical specialty would be in the 900 series. You punch it in here." He indicated rows of colored buttons. "Then the file's automatically transferred to the V bank."

"Well, this has been a fascinating tour," Mart said. "I'll make it a point to enter an appropriate commendation in the files."

The sad-faced man smiled wanly. "Well, I try to do my job..."

"Now, if you don't mind, I'll just stroll around and watch for a few minutes before I rush along to my conference."

"Well, nobody's supposed to be back here in the stacks except—"

"That's quite all right. I'd prefer to look it over alone." He turned his back on the clerk and strolled off. A glance back at the end of the stack showed the clerk settling into his chair, shaking his head.

Mart moved quickly past the ends of the stacks, turned in at the third row, followed the letters through O, N, stopped before M. He punched a button, read the name that flashed on the screen: MAJONOVITCH.

He tapped at the key; names flashed briefly: MAKISS...MALACHI...MALDON, SALLY...MALDON, MART—

He looked up. A technician was standing at the end of the stack, looking at him. He nodded.

"Quite an apparatus you have here..."

The technician said nothing. He wore a pink tag and his mouth was open half an inch. Mart looked away, up at the ceiling, down at the floor, back at the technician. He was still standing, looking. Abruptly his mouth closed with a decisive snap; he started to turn toward the clerk's desk—

Mart reached for the control knobs, quickly dialled for the eighth row, entry four; the single dot shifted into position, enlarged. The technician, distracted by the sudden move, turned, came hurrying along the aisle.

"Hey, nobody's supposed to mess with the—"

"Now, my man," Mart said in a firm tone. "Answer each question in as few words as possible. You will be graded on promptness and accuracy of response. What is the number of digits in the Technical Specialty series—the 900 group?"

Taken aback, the technician raised his eyebrows, said "Three—but—"

"And what is the specific code for Microtronics Engineer—cum Laude?"

There was a sudden racket from the door. Voices were raised

in hurried inquiry. The clerk's voice replied. The technician stood undecided, scratching his head. Mart jabbed at the colored buttons: 901...922...936 dozen three-digit Specialties into his record at random.

From the corner of his eye he saw a light blink on one of the red-painted panels; his record was being automatically transferred to the technically Qualified files. He poked the button which whirled his card from the screen and turned, stepped off toward the far end of the room. The technician came after him.

"Hey there, what card was that you were messing with...?"

"No harm done," Mart reassured him. "Just correcting an error. You'll have to excuse me now; I've just remembered a pressing engagement..."

"I better check; what card was it?"

"Oh—just one picked at random."

"But...we got a hundred million cards in here..."

"Correct!" Maldon said. "So far you're batting a thousand. Now, we have time for just one more question: is there another door out of here?"

"Mister, you better wait a minute till I see the super—"

Mart spotted two unmarked doors, side by side. "Don't bother; what would you tell him? That there was, just possibly, a teentsy weentsy flaw in one of your hundred million cards? I'm sure that would upset him." He pulled the nearest door open. The technician's mouth worked frantically.

"Hey, that's—" he started.

"Don't call us—we'll call you!" Mart stepped past the door; it swung to behind him. Just before it closed, he saw that he was standing in a four-foot by six-foot closet. He whirled, grabbed for the door; there was no knob on the inside. It shut with a decisive click!

He was alone in pitch darkness.

Maldon felt hastily over the surfaces of the walls, found them bare and featureless. He jumped, failed to touch the ceiling. Outside he heard the technician's voice, shouting. At any moment he would open the door and that would be that...

Mart went to his knees, explored the floor. It was smooth. Then his elbows cracked against metal—

He reached, found a grill just above floor level, two feet wide and a foot high. A steady flow of cool air came from it. There were screw-heads at each corner. Outside, the shouts continued. There were answering shouts.

Mart felt over his pockets, brought out a coin, removed the screws. The grill fell forward into his hands. He laid it aside, started in head-first, encountered a sharp turn just beyond the wall. He wriggled over on his side, pushed hard, negotiated the turn by pulling with his hands pressed against the sides of the metal duct. There was light ahead, cross-hatched by a grid. He reached it, peered into a noisy room where great panels loomed, their faces a solid maze of dials and indicator lights. He tried the grill. It seemed solid. The duct made a right-angle turn here. Maldon worked his way around the bend, found that the duct widened six inches. When his feet were in position, he swung a kick at the grill. The limited space made it awkward; he kicked again and again; the grill gave, one more kick and it clattered into the room beyond. Mart struggled out through the opening.

The room was brightly lit, deserted. There were large printed notices here and there on the wall warning of danger. Mart turned, re-entered the duct, made his way back to the closet. The voices were still audible outside the door. He reached through the opening, found the grill, propped it in position as the door flew open. He froze, waiting. There was a moment of silence.

"But," the technician's voice said, "I tell you the guy walked into the utility closet here like he was boarding a rocket for Paris! I didn't let the door out of my sight, that's why I was standing back and yelling, like you was chewing me out for..."

"You must have made an error; it must have been the other door there..."

The door closed. Mart let out a breath. Now perhaps he'd have a few minutes' respite in which to figure a route off Level Fifty.

13

He prowled the lanes between the vast cybernetic machines, turned a corner, almost collided with a young woman with red-blonde hair, dark eyes and a pouting red mouth which opened in a surprised O.

"You shouldn't be in here," she said, motioning over her shoulder with a pencil. "All examinees must remain in the examination room until the entire battery of tests have been completed."

"I...ah..."

"I know," the girl said, less severely. "Four hours at a stretch. It's awful. But you'd better go back in now before somebody sees you."

He nodded, smiled, and moved toward the door she had indicated. He looked back. She was studying the instrument dials, not watching him. He went past the door and tried the next. It opened and he stepped into a small, tidy office. A large-eyed woman with tightly dressed brown hair looked up from a desk adorned by a single rosebud in a slim vase and a sign reading PLACEMENT OFFICER. Her eyes went to a wall clock.

"You're too late for today's testing, I'm afraid," she said. "You'll have to return on Wednesday; that's afternoon testing. Mondays we test in the morning." She smiled sympathetically. "Quite a few make that mistake."

"Oh," Mart said. "Ah...Couldn't I start late?"

The woman was shaking her head. "Oh, it wouldn't be possible. The first results are already coming in..." She nodded toward a miniature version of the giant machines in the next room. A humming and clicking sounded briefly from it. She tapped a key on her desk. There was a sharp buzz from the small machine. He gazed at the apparatus. Again it clicked and hummed. Again she tapped, eliciting another buzz.

Mart stood, considering. His only problem now was to leave the building without attracting attention. His record had been altered to show his completion of a Technical Specialty; twelve of them, in fact. It might have been better if he had settled for one. Someone might notice—

"I see you're admiring the Profiler," the woman said. "It's a very compact model, isn't it? Are you a Cyberneticist, by any chance?"

Maldon started. "No..."

"What name is that? I'll check your file over to see that everything's in order for Wednesday's testing."

Mart took a deep breath. This was no time to panic... "Maldon," he said. "Mart Maldon."

The woman swung an elaborate telephone-dial-like instrument out from a recess, dialed a long code, then sat back. Ten seconds passed. With a click, a small panel on the desktop glowed. The woman leaned forward, reading. She looked up.

"Why, Mr. Maldon! You have a remarkable record! I don't believe I've ever encountered a testee with such a wide—and varied—background."

"Oh," Mart said, with a weak smile "It was nothing..."

"Eidetics, Cellular Psychology, Autonomics..."

"I hate narrow specialization," Mart said.

"...Cybernetics Engineering—why, Mr. Maldon, you were teasing me!"

"Well..." Mart edged toward the door.

"My, we'll certainly be looking forward to seeing your test results, Mr. Maldon! And Oh! Do let me show you the new Profiler you were admiring." She hopped up, came round the desk. "It's such a time saver—and of course, saves a vast number of operations within the master banks. Now, when the individual testee depresses his COMPLETED key, his test pattern in binary form is transferred directly to this unit for recognition. It's capable of making over a thousand yes-no comparisons per second, profiling the results in decimal terms and recoding them into the master record, without the necessity for activating a single major sequence within the master—and, of course, every activation costs the taxpayer seventy-nine credits!"

"Very impressive," Mart said. If he could interrupt the flow of information long enough to ask a few innocent-sounding directions...

A discreet buzzer sounded. The woman depressed a key on the desk communicator.

"Miss Frinkles, could you step in a moment? There's a report of a madman loose in the building..."

"Good Heavens!" She looked at Mart as she slipped through the door. "Please, do excuse me a moment..."

Mart waited half a minute, started to follow; a thought struck him. He looked at the Profiler. All test results were processed through this little device; what if...

A quick inspection indicated that the apparatus was a close relative of the desk-top units used at Applied Tech in the ill-fated Analogy Theory class. The input, in the form of a binary series established by the testee's answers to his quiz, was compared with the master pattern for the specialty indicated by the first three digits of the signal. The results were translated into a profile, ready for transmittal to the Master Files.

This was almost too simple...

Mart pressed a lever at the back of the housing, lifted it off. Miss Frinkles had been right about this being a new model; most of the circuitry was miniaturized and built up into replaceable sub-assemblies. What he needed was a set of tools...

He tried Miss Frinkles' desk, turned up a nail file and two bobby pins. It wouldn't be necessary to fake an input; all that was needed was to key the coder section to show the final result. He crouched, peered in the side of the unit. There, to the left, was the tiny bank of contacts which would open or close to indicate the score in a nine-digit profile. There were nine rows of nine contacts, squeezed into an area of one half-inch square. It was going to be a ticklish operation...

Mart straightened a hair-pin, reached in, delicately touched the row of minute relays; the top row of contacts snapped closed, and a red light went on at the side of the machine. Mart tossed the wire aside, and quickly referred to his record, still in focus on Miss Frinkles' desk-top viewer, then tickled tumblers to show his five letter, four digit personal identity code. Then he pressed a cancel key, to blank the desk screen and dropped the cover back into place on the Profiler. He was sitting in a low chair, leafing through a late issue of *Popular Statistics* when Miss Frinkles returned.

"It seems a maintenance man ran berserk down on Nine Level," she said breathlessly. "He killed three people, then set fire to—"

"Well, I must be running along," Mart said, rising. "A very nice little machine you have there. Tell me, are there any manual controls?"

"Oh, yes, didn't you notice them? Each test result must be validated by me before it's released to the Master Files. Suppose someone cheated, or finished late; it wouldn't do to let a disqualified score past."

"Oh, no indeed. And to transfer the data to the Master File, you just push this?" Mart said, leaning across and depressing the key he had seen Miss Frinkles use earlier. There was a sharp buzz from the Profiler. The red light went out.

"Oh, you mustn't—" Miss Frinkles exclaimed. "Not that it would matter in this case, of course," she added apologetically, "but—"

The door opened and the redhead stepped into the room. "Oh," she said, looking at Mart. "There you are. I looked for you in the Testing room—"

Miss Frinkles looked up with a surprised expression. "But I was under the impression—" She smiled. "Oh, Mr. Maldon, you *are* a tease! You'd already completed your testing, and you let me think you came in late...!"

Mart smiled modestly.

"Oh, Barbara, we must look at his score. He has a fantastic academic record..." She looked at the screen. "I don't remember cancelling...She dialed again. "...at least ten Specialized degrees, and *magna cum laude* in every one..."

The screen glowed. Miss Frinkles adjusted a knob, scanned past the first frame to a second. She stared.

"Mr. Maldon! I knew you'd do well, but a *perfect* score!"

The hall door banged wide. "Miss Frinkles—" a tall man stared at Mart, looked him up and down. He backed a step. "Who're you? Where did you get that suit—"

"MISTER Cludd!" Miss Frinkles said in an icy tone. "Kindly refrain from bursting into my office unannounced—and kindly show a trifle more civility to my guest, who happens to be a very remarkable young man who has just completed one of the finest test profiles it has been my pleasure to see during my service with Placement!"

"Eh? Are you sure? I mean—that suit...and the shoes..."

"I like a conservative outfit," Mart said desperately.

"You mean he's been here all morning...?" Mr. Cludd looked suddenly uncomfortable.

"Of course!"

"He was in my exam group, Mr. Cludd," the red-haired girl put in. "I'll vouch for that. Why?"

"Well...it just happens the maniac they're looking for is dressed in a similar suit, and...well, I guess I lost my head. I was just coming in to tell you he'd been seen on this floor.

"He made a getaway through a service entrance leading to the helipad on the roof, and..." he ran down.

"Thank you, Mr. Cludd," Miss Frinkles said icily. Cludd mumbled and withdrew. Miss Frinkles turned to Mart.

"I'm so thrilled, Mr. Maldon..."

"Golly, yes," Barbara said.

"It isn't every day I have the opportunity to Place an applicant of your qualifications. Naturally, you'll have the widest possible choice. I'll give you the current prospectus, and next week—"

"Couldn't you Place me right now, Miss Frinkles?"

"You mean—today?"

"Immediately." Mart looked at the redhead. "I like it here. What openings have you got in your department?"

Miss Frinkles gasped, flushed, smiled, then turned and played with the buttons on her console, watching the small screen. "Wonderful," she breathed. "The opening is still unfilled. I was afraid one of the other units might have filled it in the past hour." She poked at more keys. A white card in a narrow platinum holder with a jewelled alligator clip popped from a slot. She rose and handed it to Mart reverently.

"Your new I. D. sir. And I know you're going to make a wonderful chief!"

14

Mart sat behind the three-yard-long desk of polished rosewood, surveying the tennis-court-sized expanse of ankle-deep carpet which stretched across to a wide door of deep-polished mahogany, then swivelled to gaze out through wide windows of insulated, polarized, tinted glass at the towers of Granyauck, looming up in a deep blue sky. He turned back, opened the silver box that rested between a jade pen-holder and an ebony paper-weight on the otherwise unadorned desk, lifted out a Chanel dope-stick, sniffed it appreciatively. He adjusted his feet comfortably on the desk top, pressed a tiny silver button set in the arm of the chair. A moment later the door opened with the faintest of sounds.

"Barbara—" Mart began.

"There you are," a deep voice said.

Mart's feet came off the desk with a crash. The large man approaching him across the rug had a familiar look about him...

"That was a dirty trick, locking me in the shower. We hadn't figured on that one. Slowed us up something awful." He swung a chair around and sat down.

"But," Mart said. "But...but..."

"Three days, nine hours and fourteen minutes," the newcomer said, eyeing a fingerwatch. "I must say you made the most of it. Never figured on you bollixing the examination records, too; most of 'em stop with the faked Academic Record, and figure to take their chances on the exam."

"Most of 'em?" Mart repeated weakly.

"Sure. You didn't think you were the only one selected to go before the Special Placement Board, did you?"

"Selected? Special..." Mart's voice trailed off.

"Well, surely you're beginning to understand now, Maldon," the man from whom Mart had stolen the suit said. "We picked you as a potential Top Executive over three years ago. We've followed your record closely ever since. You were on every one of the Board Members' nomination lists—"

"But—but I was quota'd out—"

"Oh, we could have let you graduate, go through testing, pick up a green tag and a spot on a promotion list, plug away for twenty years, make Exec rank—but we can't waste the time. We need talent, Mart. And we need it now!"

Mart took a deep breath and slammed the desk. "Why in the name of ten thousand devils didn't you just TELL me!"

The visitor shook his head. "Nope; we need good men, Mart— need 'em bad. We need to find the superior individuals; we can't afford to waste time bolstering up the folklore that the will of the people constitutes wisdom. This is a city of a hundred million people—and it's growing at a rate that will double that in a decade. We have problems, Mart. Vast, urgent problems. We need men that can solve 'em. We can test you in academic knowledge, cook up psychological profiles—but we have to KNOW. We have to find out how you react in a real-life situation; what you do to help yourself when you're dumped on the walkaway, broke and hopeless. If you go in and have your brain burned, scratch one. If you meekly register to wait out a Class Two test opening—well, good luck to you. If you walk in and take what you want..." he looked around the office... "then welcome to the Club."

ANSWER
Fredric Brown

This little gem of a story concerns finding an answer to one of the most persistent questions ever asked by human beings. Men and women have been seeking an answer to this question for thousands of years. The one given by the computer in this story may shock you.

Dwar Ev ceremoniously soldered the final connection with gold. The eyes of a dozen television cameras watched him and the sub-ether bore throughout the universe a dozen pictures of what he was doing.

He straightened and nodded to Dwar Reyn, then moved to a position beside the switch that would complete the contact when he threw it. The switch that would connect, all at once, all of the monster computing machines of all the populated planets in the universe—ninety-six billion planets—into the supercircuit that would connect them all into one supercalculator, one cybernetics machine that would combine all the knowledge of all the galaxies.

Dwar Reyn spoke briefly to the watching and listening trillions. Then, after a moment's silence he said, "Now, Dwar Ev."

Dwar Ev threw the switch. There was a mighty hum, the surge of power from ninety-six billion planets. Lights flashed and quieted along the miles-long panel.

Dwar Ev stepped back and drew a deep breath. "The honor of asking the first question is yours, Dwar Reyn."

"Thank you," said Dwar Reyn. "It shall be a question which no single cybernetics machine has been able to answer."

He turned to face the machine. "Is there a God?"

The mighty voice answered without hesitation, without the clicking of a single relay.

"Yes, *now* there is a God."

Sudden fear flashed on the face of Dwar Ev. He leaped to grab the switch.

A bolt of lightning from the cloudless sky struck him down and fused the switch shut.